CALL IT HOME

PHOTOGRAPHS BY SHADE DEGGES

CLARKSON POTTER/PUBLISHERS

NEW YORK

AMBER LEWIS WITH CAT CHEN

CALL IT HOME

THE DETAILS THAT MATTER

CONTENTS

INTRODUCTION

I have always placed great value on the importance of our living spaces to our quality of life. Of course, we all know the age-old saying "Home is where the heart is," but home is also where I find inspiration, emotional security, and all-around peace. Many of us have been fortunate enough to also learn that a home can also be where we work and even where we take our "staycations." While it might start out as a structure with four walls and a roof, a home can be transformed into a place that also brings comfort.

Spending the last decade as an interior designer has truly been a joy. With my company, Amber Interiors, I found my niche, and I now have not only a career doing what I love most, but also a platform on which to share my life's work with others. I do not take this responsibility lightly, and with each new project I embark upon, I strive to create better spaces—for my clients, for myself, and for anyone following along on social media.

Still, as any designer knows, when it comes to designing a unique space—one that isn't merely a lather-rinse-repeat of the same room over and over—the struggle is real. Thanks to the Internet, we are all exposed, time and again, to images of interiors that lack that special, timeless quality that makes a space unique. Oversaturation of any one trend can make it difficult to define and hone your own style. After all, it can be hard to differentiate what everyone else is doing from what genuinely resonates with *you.*

For years, I have been homing in on my personal aesthetic and have tried to push myself creatively. But even I—a professional designer who should know better—have fallen prey to a design fad or two, only to ask myself a few years down the road, *What was I thinking?* So, in order to pull together all the elements of a space I am designing without getting caught up in passing fancies, I have learned to ask myself a few key questions:

· **Will I like this design element a decade from now?**

· **Will this design look like it was done in [insert year] or at any point over the last fifty years?**

- **Is this design a true reflection of my personal aesthetic?**
- **Does this design feel one-of-a-kind, or like something I have seen done time and time again?**

When designing a home, you find yourself asking a lot of questions like these and struggling to come up with the answers. In writing this second book, I have aimed to create a framework for simplifying this complicated process.

I want to help you find your personal style!

While I've been a professional interior designer for more than fifteen years, I've been at this design thing in one form or another for as long as I can remember. (Picking paint colors before the age of ten totally counts, right?) As with my design aesthetic and personal taste, things were quite different when I started Amber Interiors in 2011. Back then, the furniture and home spaces were dedicated mainly to the likes of national retailers, and my current design and entrepreneurial heroes were only starting to pave the way for an evolution in interior design, at least in the digital world. I started dabbling in DIY, made pillows, restored furniture—I documented everything and shared my work with whoever cared to read about it on the internet.

My approach to it all was quite simple: to be the most genuine version of myself by doing what I loved most, which was to create and design. I was starting from scratch in what was, for me, uncharted territory, and I had nothing to lose. I thought, *What could go wrong?* Well—I learned—a lot! It turns out that, when building a home, nothing is guaranteed, but you *can* hang your hat on good old Murphy's Law.

Still, you've gotta roll with the punches. As a budding designer and a hardheaded, fiercely determined person to the core, I had some lofty goals I was hell-bent on achieving. Did this happen within the timeline I hoped for? Absolutely not. Frankly, I'm still working on a few of them, and on some days, I just want to give up. It has taken years of trial and error—building a strong, dependable team and taking a few risky chances on unknowns—to get to where I am today. Above all, it was important for me to stay true to what I believed in—so,

I opted out of taking on investors. I started making moves toward immediate financial independence so that I could retain control of how my business operated, both logistically and creatively. It wasn't easy to build a business this way, but looking back on it now, I wouldn't change a thing.

I often think about my design career as a journey, one that started with a deep love of nature and the outdoors inspired by the places I visited as a child and by the California beach where I grew up. Decorating window displays in retail shops in my early twenties led me to discover myself and to focus my energies on what is now known as Amber Interiors. Then I came to the most recent and jarring milestone in my journey. In 2020, right before I turned forty, I was diagnosed with multiple sclerosis (more commonly known as MS). The diagnosis rocked my world, of course, but it also, ultimately, gave me a level of strength and perseverance I didn't know I possessed.

When I look back on that journey now, I see it as necessary to constructing the foundation for everything I currently have in my life. My experiences, good and bad, have made me who I am today. I have had to make countless tough decisions and sacrifices to get to where I am now, to experience many things, both positive and negative, until I learned to trust my instincts. This doesn't mean I get it right every time. In fact, I can promise you I don't always. My point is that you grow with your journey, and I have so much to share about mine.

If you've read my first book, *Made for Living,* you may see some noticeable differences between this book and that one. Chalk it up to evolution: I have learned so much about myself and about interior design over the past couple of years. In that earlier book, I focus on my stylistic preferences when designing a space. In these pages, I'm going to take you through the details, and specifics involved, when designing several homes.

So, let's get personal, let's talk business, and, of course, let's share design.

In this room, my client wanted somewhere to lounge without adding more sofas or chairs, so our solution was a built-in corner seat upholstered in a heavy linen that added necessary texture to the space.

THE HOWS AND WHYS

The relationships among me, my team, the clients, the architect, and the builder are the most important part of a successful house project. We all work hand in hand, usually over a span of years, to build upon what each of us designs and conceptualizes. To use an analogy, you have to treat a home construction project and the people you choose to work with the same as you would choose a team for any sport. As the saying goes, "The strength of the team is each member. The strength of each member is the team." You depend on one another, so you have to form a bond, one that involves trust and a shared goal: to build a beautiful home.

Designing interior spaces can be daunting. In this digital day and age, we have become so accustomed to seeing images of perfect homes on television and social media that it's hard to remember that the rooms in each of those pretty pictures did not get that way miraculously overnight. No, no, my friend: Every inch of those carefully curated spaces you see online required a whole lot of hard work and commitment—not to mention a team of people behind the scenes and a pretty decent budget at that.

Each of the projects I show off in this book was a years-long production involving intricate planning; worksite chaos; shopping, sourcing, and resourcing materials; budgeting; and sadly, over the last couple of years, *so many* delays. (Thanks, Covid-19!) As professional interior designers, our job is to make it look like we whipped up a space without any stress or tribulation when, in reality, this is far from the truth. But I am not here to demystify interior design, nor to sugarcoat how much work goes into building and designing homes. I do, however, want to break down the hows and whys a bit so that you can take away the most salient information and apply it to your own current or future project.

I have spent countless hours figuring out how best to use my strengths as a designer. Identifying my favorite parts of the process is easy: the very beginning and the very end. It's at these stages that I get to visualize the space (the very beginning) and then realize that vision with pieces that make a house feel like a home (the very end). It is at these moments that, I feel, I truly put my skills to the test, when I am free to be both creative *and* the most authentic version of myself.

From the moment I set foot onto a property, I enter another world. My mind goes off in a million directions, and I start dreaming and scheming, considering all the possibilities. First, I study the project from many angles. If I am walking into a home that needs a full remodel, I like to visit it at different times of day, to read the light and see what the surrounding landscape does to the property. I take note of all the original architecture and determine what should be preserved and what is no longer serving the space. If we are building a home from the dirt up, I like to feel out the land, study the sun's path throughout the day, and start determining how nature will inform the interiors. I derive so much joy from thinking about all the design possibilities.

While I'm a big-picture person, I have great respect for the process of construction and design. In our digital world, we have been conditioned to believe that beautiful spaces are easy to come by and that with no more than the snap of a finger or a transition jump in an Instagram Reel, they suddenly just appear! Spoiler alert: They don't. Even I am guilty of posting those addictive "before" and "after" videos showing how to completely transform a space in one easy, ta-da moment. And yes, they are satisfying to watch . . . but also completely unrealistic! And unfortunately, they can introduce in people's minds some absurd expectations for how long it *should* take to build a home or create a beautiful space. This is why I've decided to set the record straight and dedicate this chapter to simplifying the extremely (but realistically) long process of home-building magic.

This primary bedroom in the Beach House (page 142) was begging for twin armchairs to enjoy the view of one of California's most coveted coastlines.

FURNITURE SCALE FOR GOOD FLOW

Selecting pieces of furniture that are appropriately scaled to a room and to one another can be a challenge. When you're working with a large room, the size and scale of each piece are key to ensuring the room's flow. Here are some quick tips for meeting this challenge:

· Select furniture with an interesting shape—think an unusual arm or a unique leg design—but that has a deeper seat or a slightly higher back than normal. Even just a couple of extra inches added to the height, depth, and width of a piece can contribute to the comfort it brings.

· Pro tip: When in doubt, tape it out! Don't be afraid to pull out the tape measure and the blue painter's tape and start blocking out your potential pieces on the floor. Before making any big, permanent selections, it's helpful to imagine how the space will feel when full of furniture.

· Make sure there is enough room between furniture pieces so you won't worry about knocking something over or smacking your knee on the corner of the coffee table. There is no one rule to go by, but I typically place a coffee table at least sixteen inches away from the sofa. As for spacing between other pieces, many variables can affect furniture's position in a room. For this reason, I prefer to walk through the space and make sure it is not awkwardly laid out and that the pieces feel well placed for optimal function. Imagine yourself using the space, and be sure the layout is in line with the room's intended purpose.

In the primary bedroom of Client: Totally Beachin' we had to be deliberate about furniture scale, which required us to meticulously measure for every inch in order to squeeze in bedside storage while still achieving a clear walkway to the bathroom.

HOW TO PRIORITIZE A PROJECT

We designers always ask ourselves how we will turn an idea into a reality and why we are making this or that particular design decision. The number of moving parts can be shocking on the first go-round, so let me share some of the key steps I believe are necessary for keeping a home project on track:

Have a solid plan in place. When it comes to a design project, having a crystal-clear plan is the only way to go. As designers, we are hired to create a vision—but first, we must tell a story, in an easy-to-read format, of how the finished home will look. We have to boil the process down so it makes sense to our clients—and there is so much to make sense of. This is the value of hiring your own designer. This person will work closely with you and help you create the right plan.

Be clear on roles and responsibilities. Whether you're a professional interior designer or a homeowner, establishing clear roles for yourself and your team (or even for your family) in the early stages of any project is crucial. Make sure everyone knows who the main point of contact is for each vendor and who is paying the invoices and keeping track of the budget. If you have hired pros, know who specifically is in charge of what. What is the architect in charge of versus the builder versus the interior designer? And as the homeowner, ask how you fit into the mix.

Do not assume someone else is taking care of a task. Make it known, loud and clear, who is doing what—even if it feels obvious. Bonus points if you can establish a system of checks and balances straight out of the gate. Something that can really keep a team accountable is a biweekly check-in meeting or call.

Stay organized. As a firm, we have some fancy project management software that helps us stay on track, but you can do just fine with traditional methods, such as those I list on page 23. It helps to use frequently updated Excel spreadsheets and lots of email communication to document as much of the project as possible. In my offices, keeping a checklist and establishing deadlines

For Client: Farm in the Front . . . (page 65), the homeowners had an end goal of achieving an Old-World country manor, and they trusted me with creative freedom to bring modernity to their vision.

Think about how you want your guests to feel in your home. In the powder room of Client: Worth the Wait (page 28), we created an oasis with Calacatta countertops and floor-to-ceiling white oak paneling and styled it out with linen hand towels and fresh flowers.

are two nonnegotiable steps. For your own project, set the tone and make sure everyone is held accountable.

Be patient but persistent. The home design industry requires a lot of checking in and following up. While occasional delays are a given, be sure you're staying on top of what needs to be done and when. You'd be surprised at how much can fall through the cracks when you don't manage your project consistently. Of course, you don't want to overly pester anyone—but by establishing standard communication guidelines early on, you'll be able to keep tabs on what is happening (or supposed to be happening) from week to week.

Build a stellar team. After all, this is a group of people with whom you'll be working for a relatively long period and on whom, more than likely, you'll be spending a decent amount of money. *Do your research.* Ask for references and talk to anyone you can who has had a direct working relationship with these potential team members. Make sure to ask important questions about a contractor's communication style, billing practices, and how well they cooperate with their subcontractors. Above all, go with your gut. Learning to trust and work well with architects, builders, and designers can take time, and you might not always get it right the first go-round—which is okay.

When vetting any team member, ask yourself a few important questions:

- **Can I be collaborative and creative with this person?**

- **Do we share the same goals?**

- **Do I trust them?**

Establish the desired vibe. Heading into your project, be sure to establish the aesthetic for the space. Nine times out of ten, you'll probably decide very early on—if not before taking the first steps on the project—what you want the space to look like. This seems obvious, but you would be surprised at how easy it is to get distracted by all the options and styles out there. You don't want all these shiny objects to lure you away from what you truly want for the space.

Start by asking yourself some simple questions:

- **How do I want to *feel* in this house?**

- **How do I want my *guests* to feel when they are here?**

- **What colors make me the happiest and the calmest?**

- **What colors make me anxious? (Stay away from those.)**

- **What am I hoping to accomplish with the overall aesthetic for this home?**

- **Do I want the home to feel in line with the house's architectural style (more modern or more traditional)?**

Once you nail down some of these answers, you'll be one step closer to establishing your vibe.

When it comes to colors and materials, I am personally all about mood boards. You want to lay out everything to see what really works. This means pulling together sample materials (e.g., stone and tile samples, hardware, fabric and paint swatches) to see how it all jibes. This can be done in the early stages, when you're picking foundational elements such as flooring, countertops, and cabinets—all of which will help guide you to that perfect color palette. Don't let your mood board box you in, though. You can adjust it as the project evolves, but if you have a solid starting point, it will be much harder to deviate from it. While apps like Pinterest and Instagram can be overwhelming, they are also great tools for putting all your ideas in one place. Use them to help solidify the vibe and go from there.

In the coming chapters, I dive into nine major projects I have worked on over the last few years since the publication of my first book, *Made for Living*. Each of these homes (two of them owned by the same client) has its own story to tell, and each owner gave the team the necessary trust and time to make it happen.

This book is a grand tour of these homes. We will go from room to room, up and down staircases and in and out of kitchens and bathrooms, exploring each home inch by inch while I explain each design decision you see.

STAY ORGANIZED

Here are some helpful organizational programs I love and use on the regular.

- **Dropbox.** A secure tool that stores in one place all the documents that come with a home project, Dropbox allows you to organize folders within folders and even upload images. If you don't want to pay for extra storage, you can create a Google Drive master folder to keep everything in one place. Your goal is to store all your documents in the cloud so each member of your team can access them at any time.

- **Shared photo albums.** If you have an iPhone or any smartphone, create a shared album for the team. Because it is shared, multiple people will be able to upload photos to it. It's a great way to provide visuals of the project and view updated images. There are also ways to add comments and "thumbs-up" emoticons to whatever is shared. However, never assume that a comment or a like serves as official communication. Put your feedback in an email—and make sure you get a response.

- **Google Sheets and Docs.** Google word processing and spreadsheet programs are generally very intuitive and user-friendly; we use them in the design offices for many things. They are helpful for when many people need to see a set of documents, as they allow multiple people on a team to edit and make changes.

- **Evernote.** This app is great for task management and for keeping notes on your smartphone and computer. Use it to compile a running to-do list or as a way to keep your project on schedule.

For every home we design, including this one (Client: Houston, page 98), my design firm uses Studio Webware, which keeps track of proposals, schedules, payments, and more.

ALL GOOD IN THE NEIGHBORHOOD

A whole lot of intention goes into building a client's "forever home"—but not *only* intention. A whole lot of love and care are also spent on every single detail. One of the things I pride myself on as a designer is how much time I spend thinking about the details. I find that this is where a home can go from good to great. For me, no detail is too big or too small, and each inch should matter as much as the previous one. Anyone who knows me will say that I am simply obsessed (neurotic, even) about these special details. Be it a kitchen countertop edge or the way a drape is pleated—all of it needs to be considered.

In *Made for Living*, I share a bit about how I can go around in circles obsessing over the tiniest things. In this chapter, I share the important details that sometimes get overlooked. You can't skip going that extra mile. Taking your time to consider the details matters so much to your home's overall design aesthetic.

For the two homes I feature in this chapter, I wanted to share some examples of how tweaking even small details can dramatically change the aesthetic. The projects in this chapter happen to belong to two very different families, but when they approached us to design their homes, the general goal was the same: to create a timeless space that reflected who the clients were as individuals, but also one that accommodated plenty of family and friends and a growing brood (animals included).

CLIENT: WORTH THE WAIT

Of course, I could say this about every home, but this one in particular was a labor of love, one that took about four years to complete. (Yes, you read that right. To be fair, though, Covid-19 shut down the world a couple of years into the project, and what with the domino effect of shipping delays and viral outbreaks slowing things down week after week, it was a struggle to get it back up on its feet.) We were brought on in the early stages to help inform the overall architectural aesthetic of the project and choose all the interior and exterior finishes and, later, to furnish and decorate the entire space. The clients were a dream to work with, the perfect partners for realizing this beautiful home

You can probably imagine how hard it is to design something and set a team on the critical path forward only to be repreatedly stopped in your tracks. In construction and design, so many of the decisions are made in the early days of a project's timeline, and this project was no exception—but with Covid-19 delays added in. To ensure that the team never lost sight of the desired vibe, I continually reminded them (and even myself) of the decisions made early on. I kept asking myself if I had indeed made the right choices in interior furniture and finishes. I wanted to be sure that what we'd chosen *nearly four years earlier* was timeless, classic, and not too trendy or straying from the overall vision. Luckily, in the end, I was still very pleased with what we'd picked. In terms of square footage, this was one of the largest homes we had ever built and, naturally, required more furniture and finishes than a smaller home would—all representing decisions we had made years before and all difficult to keep track of on the stop-and-start timeline.

This family wanted an open, bright space with lots of room for their young kids to run around and enough dedicated areas for privacy when it was needed. The roughly eleven thousand square feet of living space could have felt massive and cold if the wrong materials had been chosen or if the furniture layout

We wanted the entryway to look distinct from the rest of the home, so we decided to cover the walls and ceiling with wood paneling and opted for sturdy Blue Chinois tumbled limestone for the floors.

hadn't been carefully considered. We wanted the home to have lots of natural elements, gorgeous wood tones, and layers of classic architectural details throughout. We did this by adding various styles of wall paneling and lots of ceiling details and by combining both plaster and paint on the walls for depth and dimension.

The primary bedroom suite in this home has it all. A place to lounge, sleep, bathe, take a sauna, and even work (if you must), this space was a true hideaway in the home, and our clients wanted it to feel like a staycation every day. It was important for them to have a place where they could really do it all from the comfort of their bedroom. And it came with a pretty sweet balcony with a gorgeous view of L.A.

We had some challenges on our hands when we got the plans for this area of the home. The space was quite long and narrow, so we had to make sure every corner was filled and visually interesting. A rule of thumb: Built-in furniture always makes a space feel custom designed and elevated, so we focused on adding a few key pieces tailored to this bedroom. We opted for a built-in headboard spanning the entire wall, over a typical bed frame. Its nubby-textured fabric was simple, but a paneled wall, custom burlwood nightstands, and brass sconces brightened it. We also added built-in seating along one of the corner windows, with custom tufted cushions, for the ultimate private lounge. As we did throughout the whole house, we paid close attention to the color palette, keeping the tones warm. I wanted this space to feel grounded, a bit earthy, and extremely peaceful.

Moving into the primary bathroom, we had to design a space around a checklist of things we knew we wanted to add: double water closets, his and her vanities, a sauna, a steam shower, a bathtub, and, of course, big windows so as not to miss out on the abundant natural light. We designed the space to have it all, but we made sure to focus on the elevated details to ensure that this bathroom went above and beyond for the homeowners.

We opted against using stone or tile on the floors and, instead, chose to carry the same wood used throughout the whole house into the bathroom. It provided a soft, neutral canvas for all the additional architectural elements we added in. By using warm wood tones on the cabinetry, selecting antique-brass plumbing, building a custom brass shower enclave as the focal point of the room, and choosing a deep-veined marble for the large tub surround and countertops, we kept the space grounded and gentle. We didn't miss out on the opportunity to soften the space even further by adding fabric sconce shades, a French-tufted bench cushion, and beautiful drapery behind the tub. Tonal was the theme in this primary room, and we made sure every material and color fit the bill.

The design of this home for our incredibly special client was a long journey that was ultimately, well, "worth the wait." We didn't budge on a single detail, which this home had a whole lot of, and I couldn't be happier with the finished result.

Adding multiple species and tones of wood can work in your favor. Pro tip: Choose finishes that have undertones of the same hue. With this kitchen, I made sure the island and built-in banquette had similar warmer undertones with a plain sawn white oak done in a natural, clear matte finish; I chose a darker, but still warm, wood finish for the dining chairs, which were of solid oak and elm. Using a black-and-ivory ticking stripe in high-performance fabric for the seat cushions helped to ground these pieces and differentiate the dark from the light.

This is what I call the heart of the home. Our focus was on adding warmth and interesting architectural details throughout the home. Sometimes—even when building homes from the ground up—we are handed a set of plans that need some love or that include funky details we have to work with. In this instance, our challenge was how to tie the ceiling, which lacked excitement, into the very large and open floor plan of the kitchen and family room. The solution: We used wood beams framing white oak tongue-and-groove paneling on the ceiling.

ABOVE LEFT
As I mentioned earlier, the home was rather large, but both the clients and the team did not want its size to be the focus. Instead, we wanted the eye to go straight to the rich fabrics and color palette, the beautiful surface materials and inviting flow of the spaces. By incorporating special pieces like this vintage dining table and chairs, we were able to create a lived-in feel.

ABOVE RIGHT AND OPPOSITE
We needed to design a custom piece that had the right scale to fit this rather expansive room. It served as the perfect backdrop for the dining room and became a haven for the family's entertaining bits and pieces.

ABOVE LEFT AND OPPOSITE

Built-in elements can elevate a space, adding visual layers that help fill the room. In this living space, we needed bookshelves that were in scale for the room; the only way to achieve that was with built-ins. The fireplace is a work of art in itself. We sourced a special reclaimed limestone for the mantel to lend a rustic, lived-in feel.

PREVIOUS PAGE

The living room is an entertainer's dream, set between the bar room in the far corner and the dining room. We made sure there was comfortable seating for guests to enjoy before and after a meal and, of course, a fireplace to make the setting cozy.

Our goal for the primary bedroom was to create a tranquil sanctuary that is peaceful and cozy with plenty of seating to lounge around.

We had a clear vision for this headboard, which was that it would be low and expansive. We custom built it and covered it in a wool bouclé fabric. Then we flanked it with burlwood nightstands, which contrast the soft fabric.

Not everyone wants to work in their bedroom, but this client needed a space where he could hide away and work without being disturbed. So we designed a small functional office that allowed him to sneak in the occasional early-morning email.

WORK FROM HOME ZONE

Chances are, if you didn't have a home office or some sort of work station in your home prior to 2020, you probably do now. I don't have a home office—I know, but if you knew me, you wouldn't be that surprised. I'm more of a work-at-the-kitchen-counter or curl-up-on-the-sofa kind of gal. But for all the more profesh folks out there—which, by the way, you 100 percent should be— here is some home office inspiration for you.

     The key? Good lighting, a comfy chair, and a peaceful environment. It's all about choosing the colors and the vibe to ensure you can be your best self when getting that work done.

I try to include a desk in every home, whether it's a simple setup tucked in a guest bedroom or a serious situation that calls for its own room. In that case, I make sure there's extra lounge seating involved so my clients can take a break.

ABOVE

We designed his-and-hers vanities with a few of my favorite elements: warm wood tones on the cabinetry and antiqued brass plumbing with deep-veined marble for the countertops, which is echoed in the design of the tub.

OPPOSITE

I love using wood floors in larger primary bathrooms. I know the consensus is that wet conditions in a bathroom will damage the wood, but just as with using real marble on countertops, I do not shy away from natural materials and love the added patina that results from a truly lived-in home. A beautiful rug or bath mat is often enough to prevent any significant wear and tear to the floor.

This primary bathroom had it all, including a steam shower with custom brass doors and, to the left, a sauna.

Treat your guests right. Don't let their room be an
afterthought! Our clients considered how their guests
would experience the home, making sure these rooms
would be beautiful on their own, while still feeling
tied into the rest of the home design.

BELOW

In the ensuite bathroom, we skipped the warm aged-brass plumbing and details we used in the rest of the home in favor of a traditional polished nickel finish. The change differentiated the guest suite from the rest of the home to give guests a unique experience.

OPPOSITE

This additional bedroom is a sanctuary for guests. We chose deep, earthy tones mixed with patterns and just the right number of vintage pieces to make this space feel like a home away from home.

We designed this ultimate hangout for the little ones to be right off the family room and kitchen, so it isn't too far away from the bustling part of the home. With a table for doing homework after school and a sofa and beanbag to sink into on the weekends, this space can flex with their needs.

This classic den reminds me of a speakeasy. Because this room was in the basement, we had zero natural light. Instead of fighting it, we leaned into the moodiness for a hand-me-a-glass-of-whiskey vibe. We designed a bar with the most beautiful Rosso Levanto marble countertops, which is the perfect color and material against the dark-stained white oak walls and bar. We added a mix of lighting—modern and more traditional fixtures—and the space evened out to the perfect combination of classic and contemporary.

THE KIDS ARE ALL RIGHT

I love designing spaces for children. It's the perfect opportunity, in any home, to add some fun and a bunch of character through more juvenile and less fancy design and décor selections. When I'm pulling together kids' spaces, I try to stick to the same rules I follow when designing any part of a home. I like to keep the tones and colors complementary, but when it involves kiddos, I break free from anything too simple or too sophisticated. For children, you want to encourage both a playful and a restful environment. I like to add whimsy with patterns and bolder color choices. An easy way to achieve this: Use wallpaper. It works almost every time. I love that you can experiment with so many different patterns and color combos. Pair a stripe with a floral or a paisley with a toile. As long as everything works together to your eye, and the colors play off one another, the sky's the limit!

OPPOSITE
We always take the liberty of making kids' rooms as cute as they can be, typically choosing patterned wallpapers for the entire room and adding lots of layers by way of textiles, soft textures, and pillows.

NEXT PAGE
The open layout in the family room and kitchen is one of my favorite features of this house, and this space is definitely the most popular gathering spot for the clients. It's where you'll find the big ole cozy sofa and a breakfast nook that doubles as a craft zone for the kids. The space's close proximity to the action in the kitchen required a few counter stools for hanging out.

CLIENT: FARM IN THE FRONT, LAKE IN THE BACK

These enthusiastic clients really did their homework. They loved our work as a firm and decided early on to pretty much give us free rein to do whatever we wanted—within reason, of course. Because of this creative freedom and respect for the client-designer relationship, their home has become one of my favorite projects to date. This family is a special one, a growing one, and one that was down to do it all. They gave us some guidelines and specifics unique to them, and together we started to build the team. The clients knew that if we selected the best builder out there, we could probably avoid hiring a full-time architect and just keep the design between my firm and the construction team. I had an existing relationship with Philip Posen from Ingenuity Builders, a firm with which I had completed another design-and-build project, so we reached out to them to partner with us as the construction team. The shared goal from the start was to build a quality home that was perfect for the whole gang, including kids, pets, parents, friends, and extended family.

When the clients first contacted me, they had just purchased a *very* cool home. Both the bones and the location were ideal, and the traditional-style, eight-thousand-square-foot-plus home, located on a small private lake in Los Angeles, was practically perfect. As great as the house was, though, the family felt it lacked the character they knew they wanted in a home. After some brainstorming, we put pen to paper and started planning. Thankfully, the previous owners had taken great care of the home. It just needed a fresh take on parts of the floor plan that did not work for the new homeowners and on windows and doors that didn't do enough justice to the lake views and expansive backyard. We opted to open up as many spaces as possible but to keep the original flow. The kitchen placement remained the same, and the

kids' rooms and primary bedroom suite stayed put, but we snuck in as much square footage as possible and took down some majorly distracting interior walls that rendered the spaces darker than necessary.

Once we embarked on the plans—removing walls and adding height to windows—we realized that these major changes would dramatically alter the feel of the home and how the clients experienced the space from outside in and inside out. We wanted character, layers, and warmth, but both environments needed to blend together.

When tackling such a hefty remodel, I seek to keep the interior space from feeling too disjointed in relation to the exterior style. For me, exterior vibes should set the tone for the whole home. In this case, my clients liked the house's original charm and curb appeal so much that we backed into that look with our interior design. Basically, I wanted to make sure the minimally updated exterior matched the maximally updated interior. We wanted the home to feel a bit like an English country manor, but with more contemporary elements and the addition of clean lines throughout. Having both spent years traveling the world, the homeowners love Old World/European style, so we focused on incorporating reclaimed materials and stones; adding architectural details like wood paneling and hand-hewn beams throughout; and using a combination of wallcoverings, such as decorative wainscoting, plaster, and wallpaper.

Though this home is by no means small, a lot of the square footage was originally sucked into spaces that could not actually be enjoyed in the way the homeowners wanted. The many small, winding hallways and other empty parts of the home we ultimately filled with more usable square feet. By carefully analyzing the layout, we figured out what might get the most bang for our clients' buck and made the best of what we had to work with. In the end, we didn't waste an inch of space. We even managed to squeeze in a few unexpected spaces: a secret playroom, a small gym, a tiny, updated powder room, and a walk-in pantry with a wine room. The house feels grand but extremely approachable, and the floor plan allows for great flow from space to space.

Upon entering the home, you are greeted by one of my staircase designs I cherish most. When we began the house project, the clients presented us with a list of funky elements in the existing house we needed to fix, and the original staircase in the entryway was on that list. The entryway had the potential to be a very bright and airy space, but the original staircase was dated, dark, and bulky. Once we started adding in the decorative architectural elements and installing windows on the second story to flood more light down into the entry, the original staircase felt even more awkward. Because the stairs are usually the first thing you see when walking into a home, we took this saying literally. Treating the stairs like their own work of art, we designed quite the showpiece. There are curves and paneling and the same reclaimed wood we used for flooring throughout the home. The staircase now sets the stage for how the rest of the spaces are experienced.

Just off the entry is the formal dining room. It was important to our clients to have space to seat as many guests as possible without the room feeling stuffy or unused, as is the case with some formal dining rooms. In the home's original floor plan, this room felt cramped and featured some odd architectural details, like shallow built-ins; also, some hallways ate up usable space.

One thing we definitely did not want to change was the room's original elegant curve out into the backyard. I wanted to lean into this design element by adding reclaimed beams with tongue-and-groove paneled ceilings and a custom-curved drapery rod complete with sheers to add warmth.

When it came to decorating the space, I wanted to break away from using only one light fixture, so we sourced two custom pulley-style pieces instead. I love how they spread across the table, and I like the addition of the fabric shades for texture and interest. By adding a more contemporary piece of artwork (this one by Tyler Guinn) to the wall above the buffet console and using reupholstered vintage dining chairs paired with a vintage dining table, we managed to strike a balance between a look that feels at once old and new.

I am a big believer in restful bedrooms, especially when it comes to the primary suite. I wanted to create a space that was a reprieve from the homeowners' chaotic lives. Our clients wanted just that: a place that was quiet, calming, and restorative but also one that provided privacy from their young kids. The wife and mama bear of the family was adamant about keeping TV out of the bedroom, but because she is by no means a dictator, she wanted a space where her husband, the papa bear, could hide away and sneak in some TV time and where the two could escape as a couple. Tasked with creating such a space within the existing floor plan, we opted to make the primary suite a bit smaller. What we created was a beautiful, wood-clad room that has taken on quite a few names: "Love Lounge," "Shag Shack," "Fondle Fort" . . . The list goes on. The result is snug and comfy—just the right spot for our clients to relax together and tuck themselves away for some screen time.

We really went all out on the primary bathroom. The room was long and narrow, which presented a host of challenges as we tried to fit into it all the couple's needs. They wanted a steam shower separate from the regular shower and a bathtub. Ample storage was also key: They wanted double vanities and everything hidden away in drawers so they wouldn't have to see any "stuff on the counters." We were thrilled with how the space turned out.

All in all, the end result of this major gut remodel feels special. It is all the things our clients asked for, and the wonderful collaboration among the team members made for a smooth process. The spaces are warm and inviting and all function perfectly for the family that now calls this place home—a home that will only get better the more it is lived in.

The ceiling in the room was vaulted, and we wanted to draw attention to the height and its beauty, so we enhanced the ceiling's architectural details with wood paneling and hand-hewn beams for interest.

The corner breakfast nook was a sweet addition to the room for those smaller dinner parties or a homework station for the kids during the day. We incorporated sheer café curtains for another necessary layer and textural element.

While we wanted plenty of seating in this family room, we went "fewer but bigger" to avoid visual clutter: a chaise sofa, lounge chair, and two easily movable stools are all this room needs.

STEP IT UP

Here's another example of one element of a house where we shouldn't scrimp on style or the nitty-gritty details. In a few instances, my client's staircase was in the home's entryway—in which case, it assumed the role of creating a good first impression for their guests. In other projects, the stairs were, in many ways, its backbone. We have experimented with so many styles—from traditional to more modern, and from clean and sleek to rustic and charming. I'm talking everything from hand-wrapped leather railings to pretty welded metal ones to perfectly mismatched vintage kilim runners lining the treads. When it comes to choosing your own staircase style, take a look at the many options and don't be shy about letting your style shine, even on the stairs!

PREVIOUS PAGES
I hate to play favorites, but this staircase is very high up on my list. Situated at the entry of the house, the staircase was our chance to make a showstopping first impression on guests as they step through the door. We chose natural oak for the newel post and handrail and round wrought iron for the balusters; we used wood treads and risers to match the rest of the home's flooring.

ABOVE AND OPPOSITE
We kept the color palette for this home very warm
to retain the cozy, naturalist vibe. By staying away
from cooler tones and harsh white walls, we achieved
saturated and calming spaces throughout.

PREVIOUS PAGE
This may be the official "formal" dining room, but
our clients wanted to make sure it wasn't stuffy or
separated from the rest of the house. We chose two
custom pulley-style pendants with fabric shades,
reupholstered vintage chairs, and floor-to-ceiling
curtains to add warmth to the room.

OPPPOSITE
We landed on a beautiful slab of Taj Mahal quartzite
for the kitchen countertop. Although light in color,
this famously durable stone has minimal veining.
Scratches can, of course, happen, but they are a lot
less visible with this material, which tends to be less
finicky than marble.

PREVIOUS PAGES
One of the simplest and most elegant details of this
kitchen is the range hood. Its subtle shape draws your
attention, and the clean lines of the plaster hood is a
great example of "less is more."

This walk-in pantry was meant to be a statement in the kitchen. Not only was it entirely functional with lots of storage space, including plenty of cabinets and open shelving, we also added brick as a new element to differentiate this area. The pantry itself was enclosed with painted wood doors, and we even carved out space for a secret wine room with leather and brass racks.

From the primary bedroom's entry hall to the way we covered the existing tiny windows with custom white oak shutters, no detail in this house was overlooked. We deliberately kept the textiles neutral, and we matched the tone of the plaster walls to the bed upholstery and the bedding. For a hit of pattern, we went with a pair of horizontally striped pillows.

We created this bedroom nook so the clients could have a hideaway for watching TV or just enjoying each other's company sans children. The wall paneling and built-in sofa, upholstered in the softest fabric ever, make for an intimate, cozy space.

When it came to the primary bathroom, we went all out. The room was long and skinny, which presented a host of challenges for fitting all their must-haves into a tricky space. They wanted a steam shower that was separate from the regular shower, as well as a bathtub and double vanities with lots of drawers to keep things off the counters. Ample storage was key, so the vanities and additional cabinets were a priority. We wanted the bathtub to be different, so we chose a plaster finish, which made it stand out ever so subtly.

In one of the kids' rooms, we chose cute wallpaper
and all the sweetest patterns, and then layered them
on top of one another. Add in wicker elements and
vintage sconces, and this little girl's room turned out
to be a dream come true.

In the little girl's sweet-as-can-be bathroom, we designed inset cabinetry with a radius edge detail, which we painted, and added fluted door and drawer fronts. The honed Calacatta marble countertops feature an ogee edge.

CLEAN WORK MAKES THE DREAM WORK

A leading design ethos of mine is that just because a space is meant to be used a lot, it does not mean you need to compromise on design or style. In fact, making a useful space beautiful is one of my favorite design challenges. It is into these spaces that my clients and their loved ones—sometimes kids with muddy shoes and pups with dirty paws—trudge after a long day. So, I always pick sturdy materials and include the most functional of elements, like ample storage, hooks for coats, and cubbies for dirty shoes and boots. For several of the mudrooms we've designed, we opted for easy-to-clean flooring, like limestone. Before you commit to materials in a utility space, ask your vendor or designer how they will hold up after years of heavy use.

This mudroom in Client: Farm in the Front, Lake in the Back (page 65) is both beautiful and extremely useful, with storage for odds and ends, shelves for objets, a limestone sink, and a reclaimed wood countertop for washing muddy paws or arranging flowers.

CLIENT: HOUSTON,
WE DON'T HAVE A PROBLEM

This was a unique project because it may have been the only one in recent memory that wasn't either a teardown or a very heavy gut remodel. We had worked with this family (and the family's family) for years and knew we could meet their goals for this project with a few minor yet impactful updates. The home is located in one of the older, more charming neighborhoods in Houston, Texas. On our first visit, I experienced a special feeling driving up and down the surrounding streets, and I decided to borrow for the home some of its neighbors' old splendor while giving it my own twist.

Our clients wanted to retain the home's existing charms (like the original floors), but a few spaces (the bathrooms and fixtures) needed a facelift. The overall structure of the home, with its unique arches and original stucco-plastered walls, was beautiful. We just needed to find the right pieces to match the space. When it came to furnishings, though, we pretty much started from scratch, searching long and hard for the perfect mix of vintage furniture and new. Every piece you see in the living room, dining room, and bedrooms was added to freshen up the space.

This is one of those projects that illustrates the saying "A little goes a long way." Drastic changes don't always solve the problem. Sometimes, working with what you have but slightly altering it can make a huge difference.

Upstairs, we turned the primary bedroom into a sanctuary for our clients, who have very young children. We kept the original walls, adding a fresh coat of paint, and retained the original ceilings.

Given that we were working with the home's original architecture, we had to find ways to let in the light since the house did not have huge windows. We stuck with a palette that mixed lighter upholstery fabrics with richer wood finishes to help complement the warm white walls and add depth to the wood tones on the floors and furniture. We incorporated plenty of elements to soften the home like shearling and bouclé furniture and plush drapery. And of course, we added touches of patinated leather accents throughout the home for this Texan family. The most, dare I say, modern pieces in the home came through in the lighting, where we wanted to splash some contemporary coolness onto an otherwise traditional-style home.

Upstairs in the primary bedroom, we opted to turn this suite into a sanctuary (as we so often do for our clients who have little kiddos). We wanted the homeowners to have quiet space where the two of them could escape from time to time. The room had vaulted ceilings, so we opted for a four-poster bed, with the coziest layers, and took advantage of the extra space in the room by creating a seating area tucked perfectly by the windows. The vintage Mario Bellini "Bambole" chairs were recovered in the softest bouclé fabric that our clients could sink into after a long day.

Over in "her" bathroom, we created the ultimate Zen space for this mama. We're talking a stand-alone tub, a vanity with the prettiest slab of Calacatta marble, and a big ole shower with a pretty, natural-toned Zellige tile in a herringbone pattern. In contrast, over in "his" bathroom, we went with a bolder, more utilitarian style across the board. We got our hands on an epic slab of Borghini marble with very dark black, gray, and gold veining. We used this marble for the vanity tops and applied the full slabs to the shower walls, which we paired with custom steel doors and a darkened brass Waterworks shower system. The two bathrooms are mighty different and speak to the clients' specific aesthetic preferences, but they're also designed to perfectly complement each other.

All in all, this family home was cozy, comfortable, and classic with just the right balance of buzzworthy elements.

ABOVE AND OPPOSITE
We kept the original stucco-plastered walls and gorgeous arches but made sure to mix in modern lighting and vintage furniture to give this living room an edge.

NEXT PAGES
We hunted near and far for the perfect vintage pieces to fill this home, from the coffee and console tables to chairs that we reupholstered and vintage mirrors that we layered throughout.

LET'S GET PLASTERED

When it comes to wall finishes, I love to experiment with different textures and colors.

Plaster and other special, non-paint wall finishes are not new to the design world, but they have certainly made a comeback over the past few years. For anyone experimenting with plaster for the first time, let me offer a few tips and some of my favorite colors and brands:

· In comparison with flat paint, plaster can be a bit hard to apply, so consider hiring a craftsman who is comfortable working with it.

· The color of plaster can change based on the number of coats and how they're applied. Be patient and wait to see how it dries before you judge it.

· Look for Roman Clay from Portola Paints and Glazes. I love their Figueroa and Piano Room hues, too.

OPPOSITE
This foyer to the stairs in the Boardwalk House (page 120) features Texston plaster in Super Lucito, adding just enough subtle texture to catch the eye.

NEXT PAGES
This dining room is simple yet moody. The different wood tones from beams to table to buffet, and the weathered leather chairs, give this room a lived-in feel. It's nothing too fancy or over the top, but it's a mercurial space where our clients can gather friends and family over an evening of dinner and a whole lot of chatter.

The primary bedroom is an oasis for our clients. Our goal was to create the ultimate respite for these parents, while going for a traditional yet slightly modern feel. From the solid oak canopy bed to plush floor-to-ceiling drapery to vintage Mario Bellini chairs that we reupholstered in an ivory bouclé fabric, and layers upon layers of cozy bedding, we achieved exactly what our clients needed to achieve maximum relaxation.

A PLACE TO SOAK

OPPOSITE CLOCKWISE FROM TOP LEFT
Consider a freestanding tub when you want to make a statement in the bathroom. All of these tubs are freestanding and made of different materials: concrete, deep-veined marble, plaster, and a double-ended style in gloss white.

PREVIOUS PAGES
This is "her" primary bathroom, and it's everything our mama client dreamed of. She wanted it to be full of natural light and have a massive soaking tub and a big and bright vanity. We softened the entire room with drapery, an element I love adding to bathrooms.

Fun fact: Until recently, I absolutely hated baths. I'm not sure what changed my mind, but I am a newfound lover of tubs. Still, my hatred for baths never stopped me from designing some pretty sweet bathrooms and tubs for my deserving clients (because most other people enjoy them). Looking back on all the bathrooms we designed, I found it was the range in types of tubs we got to install and customize that made my tub-obsessed self smile from ear to ear. From plaster tubs to copper tubs to built-ins—we have experimented with all sorts of styles. I can't choose one I love more than any other, and that's all right. So, here you have it: a tub for every kind of person and style!

BEACHSIDE RETREATS

I am a California girl through and through. I've lived in the state basically all my life, and while I hate to reveal my geographic biases, it really is one of the most beautiful places on Earth. I have always admired the fact that you can drive three hours in any direction and be in a completely different topographical environment. You can stand atop a rocky cliff above the Pacific Ocean or stroll for miles on pristine sand beaches. You can go for a hike in the High Sierra or take a drive for hours across the desert and find Joshua trees. This widely varying landscape has always inspired me and was what informed the deep-seated principle I follow when creating spaces: Our surroundings should influence how we design our homes.

In this chapter, I talk about seaside living. When it comes to the coastline, not all beach climates are the same. The homes in this chapter are located six hours away from each other on the West Coast. One is centrally located, in Carmel, and the other is down south, in Newport Beach. The climates in these places are dramatically different. While Carmel is quite chilly and prone to heavier coastal winds and dramatic layers of fog, Newport Beach has more of that quintessential perfect California sunshine with horizon line sunsets. So, we designed with these climates in mind.

CLIENT: NEVER LEAVIN' 'CAUSE THE VIEWS ARE SO FREAKIN' PLEASIN'

I can say with almost 100 percent certainty that this is one of the most beautiful, not to mention coveted, plots of land on the West Coast and—dare I say it?—maybe even in all of America. In one pinch-me moment in 2017, I was contacted by esteemed architect Luca Pignata of Backen and Backen to collaborate on the design and ground-up build for this phenomenal estate located on the bluffs of Carmel, California. For this project, we set out to create not one but *two* homes for a very big and quickly expanding family. Each house was to serve a different purpose: one for the adult kids and grandkids and the other for the parents.

So, let's get the lay of the land!

We refer to the home for the clients' grown kids as the Boardwalk House, and it faces north. While there are stunning ocean views in the background, the main picture-perfect views here are of the famed Pebble Beach golf course. The other home, for the clients, was designed to face west, and we refer to it as the Beach House. This beauty is situated directly on an ocean bluff with 180-degree whitewater views. Depending on whom you ask, you may get a different opinion on which view is better. Let me be clear: Both are unreal!

The priority while planning and designing these spaces was to focus on the surrounding environment and our job was to pick materials, finishes, and furnishings that complemented not only the architecture, but also the beautiful seaside landscape.

The challenge we faced early on was how to make each house feel different but also somewhat connected. In many ways, we designed the two homes on the property as one big house with similar elements within but, somehow, different moods entirely. The materials and style were consistent throughout both homes but were distinguishable enough to give each of the two dwellings its own unique personality.

THE BOARDWALK HOUSE

This home is a dream. Upon walking into the entry vestibule, you take in the most exquisite views, and we didn't want to distract from that gorgeous backdrop when choosing furnishings and décor for the space. We clad the very tall ceilings in white oak and stained them as natural a color as possible. The architect, Luca Pignata, designed giant steel-and-glass pocket doors that slid completely into the wall so that when they were fully open, the clients could enjoy the indoor/outdoor space created. The flooring was custom white oak selected with simplicity in mind. We intentionally chose flooring that did not have many knots or heavy graining. For texture and color variation, we chose a warm, custom white plaster for the walls.

Because this house was for "the kids," we made sure to select furnishings for the main living, kitchen, bedroom, and dining spaces to complement the open-feel layout while also being durable and user-friendly. Every textural element in the house was kept tonal and earthy so as not to compete with the serenity of the outdoor surroundings. It was important to adopt a color palette that accentuated and picked up all the natural tones of the property, like the mossy greens of the trees and the sea foam blues of the ocean. Everything we added—from the flooring tiles to the ceilings to the wall treatments—had that lived-in, comfortable, approachable quality that is the cornerstone of my design aesthetic. Our clients wanted a sleeker, more modern feel to this home, and that is exactly what we gave them.

The layout of this house was long and narrow. When the architect was designing it, the clients expressed a desire for a separation between the main entertaining space and the bedrooms, which were all—with the exception of the top-floor primary suite—on the same story.

Because the kitchen/dining room is just so pretty, let's start there. I've mentioned that the clients' family was big and getting bigger each year, so we needed to accommodate enough

seating for a giant brood. Comfort was obviously important, but the clients didn't rule out furniture with a patina and some history. We opted to use vintage Pierre Jeanneret cane dining chairs with custom pads in a durable performance fabric on the seats. The giant walnut dining table was also custom-made. If you look hard enough, you'll notice we opted to go darker on the wood tones for the coffee table and dining table and chairs. This was intentional, as we had so many lighter oak finishes throughout the rest of the home. The layer of depth these pieces add nicely juxtaposes all the lighter architectural elements and upholstery.

When selecting the finishes for the kitchen, we wanted to stay with white oak for the cabinetry. We kept the materials simple and natural: light marble counters, leather barstools, and brass plumbing fixtures. We also wanted the kitchen to have a gorgeous textural element, so we chose a glazed-brick tile in a warm white to line the range hood. It offers a nice break from the plaster and doesn't feel out of place with all the other architectural elements.

The bedrooms were designed to reflect the home's overall neutral, user-friendly theme, and they are nothing short of gorgeous. There are built-in bunk beds for the kids and additional guest bedrooms for the grown-ups.

The peaceful primary suite took up the entire top floor and was therefore a bit away from the guest suites. With such gorgeous views at their disposal, the clients knew the importance of creating a room from which they could see it all. Here, we used fabrics that were simple but interesting and bedding and accessories that felt more on the spare side. With so much to see outside, less was definitely more.

Fun backstory: One big design challenge we faced with the Boardwalk House was the primary bathroom. One of the home's most notable features were those giant walls of moveable steel and glass. While beautiful, they posed some practical challenges we had to tackle—the biggest being how to provide privacy and block light while never losing sight of the views. It took some creativity, but by opting to install drapery on a motorized track, we were able

to prevent golfers on the eleventh hole from seeing inside. When closed, the drapes wrap all the way behind the sink vanity and the shower enclosure glass. This fixed the light and privacy issues, but our clients still wanted a shower with a view. So, how did we provide it? Opaque window film to the rescue! A window tinting company we work with installed the film from the floor to neck height, thus obscuring the view from the outside but allowing anyone in the shower or the bathroom to enjoy the outdoor beauty. And by creating a blended effect at the top of the tinted shower glass, we softened the transition from clear glass to opaque. The room is now a perfect example of how form and function can complement each other beautifully.

Architect Luca Pignata had a vision for this fireplace. He wanted steel windows facing the bedroom wing of the house and an incredible garden that separated the spaces. There was not a bad view from any part of this house, so we chose furniture that felt quiet, which complemented the powerful architectural elements.

The living room in the Boardwalk House was the ultimate hangout spot in this home. It was the goal, ours and the architect's, to make sure this room had the most impressive views of famed Pebble Beach.

The dining room and kitchen were part of the open-concept layout of the house. We knew how much our clients wanted to entertain visiting friends, so we designed two kitchen islands—yes, two! That may seem crazy, but we wanted family and friends to have enough room to hang in the kitchen without getting in each other's way. The dining room was subtle in color and design, with just the right amount of texture and wood tones to not distract from the outside views of the home.

Each bedroom shared design elements with the others. From the kids' bunk room to the primary bedroom to the guest rooms, we kept the materials consistent throughout, leaning into a more modern look with a lot of light oak slatted cabinetry with super clean lines. As a result, we like to think that anyone would feel comfortable sleeping in this bunk room.

I CALL TOP BUNK

I have somehow gotten very lucky with my clients. They have had either lots of kiddos or lots of grandkids, all of whom required lots and lots of bunk space. There is something about designing a bunk room that makes you want to revert to your childlike self and ask, *What would I want my room to look like if I were a little kid again?* I didn't shy away from mixing all sorts of patterns, as designing a bunk room is, at its core, about creating an environment that feels fun. And let's just say, I had way too much fun designing these rooms over the years, and I'm pretty sure if I were to take a poll of my clients' kids and grandkids, I'd find some very happy campers!

Whether you go with single beds or doubles for your bunk, pile them with pillows and blankets for ultimate comfort. For the finishing touches, a reading light is a must for each level, and built-in shelves at the head of the bed hold a good book or cup of water.

We had to find a clever way to hide closets and add more storage to a clutter-free room. Just behind those slatted white oak doors are drawers, hanging space, and perfectly measured slots for large luggage.

With its canopy bed, the primary suite takes on a beautiful, romantic feeling. The drapery was designed to encircle the entire room, covering even the floor-to-ceiling doors and windows.

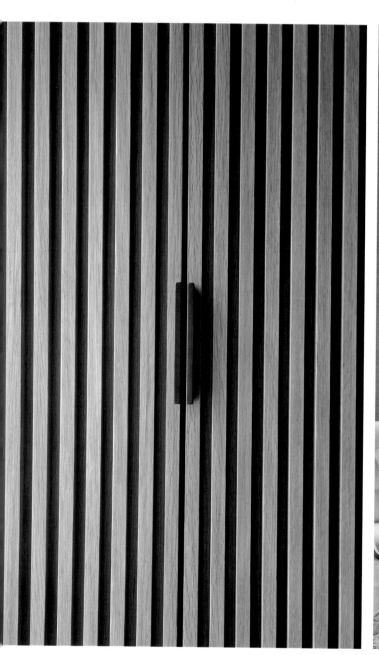

SHINE ON

When it comes to finishes for both plumbing and hardware, I am a lover of antiqued brass, which patinas so nicely every single time. I am also in love with polished nickel, which, to me, has a classic and timeless feel. I am not going to lie; I am a sucker for Waterworks plumbing and use their incredible products in most of the homes we design. Choosing plumbing and hardware can be overwhelming, but my general rule is that antiqued brass, oil-rubbed bronze, or polished nickel is a good choice every time.

PREVIOUS PAGE
The bathroom vanity floated off the steel-and-glass doors, and the back of it could be seen from the outside. Because the plumbing emerged from the floor, it needed to be hidden within the vanity legs in a clean, slick way. With our partners in the trades applying their veteran skills on this piece, we ended up with a vanity that looked perfect from all four sides. To prevent a similar problem with the floating mirrors above the vanity, we ensured that both sides of the mirrors were finished during their manufacture.

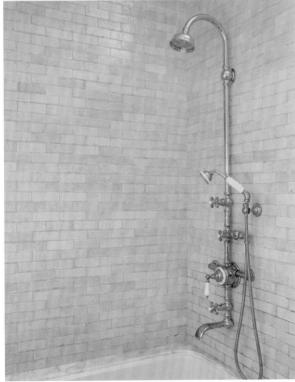

THE BEACH HOUSE

Now, moving to the west, you'll find the Beach House, which sits perched above a cliff with white sand beaches and crystal blue waters below. When you walk through the front door, you are immediately greeted not only by a stunning and grand entry and living room, but also one of the most magnificent views imaginable. The architectural design of this entrance was meant to stun, and that's exactly what Pignata and his team accomplished. Because the views here are so remarkable, low ceilings or anything but steel and glass would have taken away from the impressive outdoor landscape. So, amid the high ceilings and floor-to-ceiling steel-and-glass doors, we incorporated neutral but interesting architectural elements to help define the spaces. There is a beautiful relationship between the scale of everything inside and the vast ocean outside. The Pacific is captivating, and it made sense to match its grandeur with the interiors.

For the Beach House, I applied the same philosophy and design approach I took with the Boardwalk House. I wanted the furniture to feel inviting and interesting while not taking away from the big blue ocean outside. Counterintuitively, for this house I shied away from adding anything too stereotypically "beachy." This meant steering clear of a lot of blue hues and avoiding furnishings that felt too thematic. Attempting to re-create the beach inside the house would have distracted from the existing powerful color palette outside. Instead, I chose elements that were warm in color: beautiful muted brown and rust tones mixed with ivory- and sand-colored natural linens, with pops of leather and contrasting wood tones. They all felt wonderful in the space.

For both houses, we selected lighting and furnishings that were contemporary but never too starkly modern or precious. By mixing in warm antiqued brass on the decorative lighting above the dining table, we tied in the brass finish we had peppered throughout the home for plumbing, hardware, and other details.

When it comes to a home that skews modern, it's all about striking the right balance among clean lines, soft textures, and

subtle silhouettes. When selecting the furniture for this project, we knew that, in order to soften all the sharp angles and hard materials (steel, glass, stone, and wood), we would need to choose pieces that felt inviting. They needed to be interesting but not so much so that they upstaged the view or the architecture.

I brought the outdoors inside by using an obscure design method: Instead of directly interpreting "beach," I deconstructed it—perhaps an unexpected approach, but one that resulted in a timeless design rooted in this home's specific location (rather than a generic beachy vibe). The sand on the beach below is almost completely devoid of any specific color; it's a true neutral. For this reason, we matched the overall color scheme—furnishings, rugs, and drapery—to this sandy tone. We took inspiration from the big pieces of driftwood lining the shore by choosing colors for the upholstery that brought out the white and gray of these perfectly sun-bleached limbs. The cliffs and the rocks are jagged, but the cypress trees and the tumbled beach rocks are soft against this harsher background, and our soft furnishings and houseplants in a room filled with hard materials mimicked this juxtaposition.

I mentioned earlier that the Boardwalk House was for the clients' grown kids and that what we referred to as the Beach House was for the parents. When we were designing the latter, we needed to create a living space that struck a balance between being a place to entertain family and friends and being comfortable enough to serve as the getaway it was designed to be. The primary suite happened to be just that sanctuary. The room, located at the end of a long teak, steel, and glass corridor, was alluring, not only for the second story's gorgeous views, but also for how quiet and private it felt. When it came to the furniture and fabrics for the space, we chose to lean into the room's function as a place for chilling out, selecting very soft textures and repeating our ivory-and-sand-toned palette. The room features a perfect little seating area with some low-profile shearling-upholstered armchairs and a beautiful wood-and-bouclé

fabric king-size bed. We went with some custom bedside sconces for the lighting and a custom white-oak-and-brass side table with a single drawer for hiding built-in electrical outlets. We wanted to ensure nothing cluttered this most restful environment.

When we got to selecting materials for the primary bathroom suite, choosing elements that felt serene and calming was our modus operandi. We kept the same wood flooring for the primary suite as in the rest of the house and opted not to go with tile here. Whenever we use hardwood in bathrooms, there is generally some pushback from clients. But rest assured—wood in a bathroom is a great thing! Does it require a bit more care? Well, sure, but I promise it is nothing you can't handle. Yes, the flooring should be kept dry, but this can be accomplished with a waterproof sealer, which will inhibit mold and prevent any damage to the wood.

It's hard to look at this bathroom and not obsess over the custom-carved Nero Marquina black marble bathtub—the focal point of the space and star of the show. (This tub had to be placed inside the space while the house was under construction so it could be hoisted by crane through the still-open walls. Had we not anticipated this in our plan, the clients might have had to take their baths outdoors!) We designed the sink vanities with ample storage underneath and a six-inch marble apron front on the counters.

Taking a page from the Boardwalk House, we designed the bathroom mirrors to float over the wall of windows and applied the same opaque window film for privacy. By selecting an oil-rubbed bronze finish for the plumbing fixtures, we were able to tie them in with the dark steel window and black marble bathtub.

PREVIOUS PAGE
This is the first room our clients and their guests walk into upon entering the Beach House. Ours and the architect's goal was to capture the expansive and stunning views of the ocean and cypress trees.

The dining room and kitchen skewed on the modern side, and we rounded out the clean lines with soft silhouettes and fabrics on the dining chairs and with a vintage rug.

This area of the home was designed to be the central gathering point, with the kitchen, dining area, seating area, and a bar (not pictured), just to the right of the sitting area. We created a space for our clients to relax in a more casual setting while stirring a cocktail and enjoying the views.

Built-ins are one of my favorite ways to incorporate seating into a home, particularly as a breakfast nook or a comfy spot to relax. There's something about a custom-fit sofa or a banquette that elevates a space. I always opt for a mix of materials, textures, and fabrics, and I love using small details like leather straps or tufted cushions for visual interest. And, of course, pillows—I add lots of pillows for comfort.

The entryway and stairwell showcased the architect's and my team's vision to bring the outdoors into the space. The stone on the walls and floors was the main material we carried throughout the house, but even with its ragged edges, we managed to soften the entire space with furnishings and textiles.

ABOVE AND OPPOSITE

This primary bedroom may hold one of the top spots for spectacular views. The room is surrounded by floor-to-ceiling windows and doors that look onto the ocean and cypress trees, which also help the room stay incredibly private.

NEXT PAGES

The primary bathroom suite features a stunning custom-carved Nero Marquina black marble bathtub, which is the focal point of this room. To keep it consistent with the Boardwalk House, we designed the bathroom mirrors to float over the wall of windows and applied the same opaque window film for privacy.

The guest room and bathroom are designed similarly to the primary suite, which boasts special second-story views through floor-to-ceiling windows and, once again, floating mirrors above the vanities so guests can marvel at the views and nature surrounding them.

We carried the theme of the windows and ceilings throughout the home, but each room took on a slightly different feel by way of furniture and fabrics. Our goal for each room was to make each guest feel as if they were on vacation in their private bungalows with patios.

CLIENT: TOTALLY BEACHIN'

Building the right design and renovation team is an essential step in any home redesign. The quality of the team can make or break a project. You can waste time, energy, and money if you end up working with the wrong people. When it comes to this next project, I have to boast about the team I got to work with— the perfect blend of clients; a talented builder, Neil Longman; and the most epic architect and collaborator, Eric Olsen. Before I highlight all the things that went right and why, I want to give a big shout-out to this team. They made this multiyear experience so much sweeter.

I have worked with Olsen before, but this project was particularly enjoyable. His attention to (such gorgeous) detail throughout the entire home was impressive. Olsen and I had our hand in selecting the majority of the finishes, from plumbing and tile to wood tones and beyond. He was always willing to think things through with me creatively and entertain alternative points of view—which is how many great projects are born. He genuinely trusts our process as much as we trust his.

It was Olsen who bore the brunt of dealing with the homeowners association (HOA) in this gated community and who designed the incredibly beautiful shell we had to work with. Not unlike with our client Never Leavin' 'Cause the Views Are So Freakin' Pleasin' (page 119), we opted for a neutral color palette to let the architecture shine.

Let's start downstairs and work our way up.

With floor-to-ceiling glass doors and giant steel-framed windows, this home ran the risk of feeling cold—had we not infused the walls with washed brick and the ceilings with white oak. Because the color on the ceiling beams and paneling was so similar to the color of the wood floors, we opted to install the floors in a herringbone pattern, creating a visual separation between the two horizontal planes. To keep the spaces simple but visually textural, we went with a custom warm white plaster

finish on the more expansive walls and hallways throughout the home. While the majority of the architectural design for this home was mostly contemporary, there were definitely a lot of traditional elements included. We brought the natural stacked brick from the exterior inside, too, for a unique architectural addition to the walls, and designed a custom-aged brass stove hood to draw the eye and provide a beautiful focal point to ground the kitchen. The light fixtures feel modern but, with blown glass and a warm brass finish, incorporate some softer, more classically traditional materials.

A home should make you feel something when you walk into it, and we wanted the vibes in this home to be "approachable." In the living room, the beautiful and comfortable ivory-colored sofa we chose helps keep the room feeling light and bright. We grounded the space with darker accents (earth-toned pillows and vessels) and with a long ebonized oak side table to display more décor and books. But the main function of this room was comfort, comfort, comfort. So, we made sure to fill the space with large, cozy seating.

The dining room strikes the perfect balance between modern elegance and vintage charm. We incorporated a large slab of honed travertine along the walls to break up the expanse of plaster, giving the walls an elevated, modern feel. To add even more texture, we paired an oak dining table with leather-backed dining chairs with rush seats and custom ivory cushions. For the cluster of alabaster wall sconces, we skewed more modern. They are the perfect grounding element for a room with an otherwise relaxed feel.

The second floor of the home features all the family's bedrooms. For the primary bedroom, our clients wanted a peaceful, more traditional-style room, one that allowed natural light to flow in from every angle. Unique to the home are this room's walls: we switched things up by adding "picture frame" molding and paneling detail, which lent the space that more traditional look you find in classic European design. Mimicking the downstairs, the herringbone-patterned floor is consistent throughout the room, adding to that traditional feel. We grounded the room with a luxurious plush rug,

added a tufted upholstered bed in a beautiful ivory fabric, and included the softest layers for the bedding, which make for the coziest room.

This is one of those bathrooms that stops you in your tracks. Most of the home has ceilings of relatively "normal" height, but to add some drama to this room, we chose a high-vaulted ceiling. It not only made the space feel grand, but also allowed lots of natural light to flow into it. We carried modern elements into the space in the wall-to-wall steel-framed windows and custom-designed white oak reeded cabinetry for the vanities. Pair all that with veiny marble countertops, inset mirrors lined with antique brass, a Waterworks tub and fixtures, some funky light fixtures, a clean wooden ceiling and beams, and a massive vintage rug—and you get that perfect mix of old and new I'm always working to achieve.

Now, on to the third floor. If this doesn't scream "Southern California paradise," I don't know what does. And if this floor of the house doesn't automatically give away my clients' love of a good time, then we missed the mark! What with the (pretty epic) bar, pool table and hot tub (neither is pictured), and the outdoor chill zone/workspace, I'd say this is the best rooftop hangout imaginable. That's not even to mention the ocean views. See? Not too shabby!

OPPOSITE
Antique brass plumbing against white oak wood with marble countertops adds a splash of drama with a black stove and brass vent hood—it's a look I'll never get tired of.

PREVIOUS PAGE
We found the perfect juxtaposition from the steel-framed, floor-to-ceiling windows with bright and plush furniture as the focal point in the living room. The home has a more modern feel, but we wanted to soften the entire space and create an approachable atmosphere.

We chose washed brick for the walls, white oak for the ceilings, and a herringbone-patterned floor to create a visual separation between the two horizontal planes.

The dining room features a large slab of honed travertine along the lower wall, with a built-in fireplace, to keep this space feeling snug and relaxed for dinner parties. We chose natural elements—oak and leather—for the table and chairs, and added a bit of modern with a cluster of alabaster wall sconces and a brass pendant.

For this staircase, we achieved a clean, smooth look by designing the handrails to turn into the newel post in one continuous piece. This is a three-story home, so the staircase played a major role in the overall design of the space.

The primary bedroom leans more traditional with classic European design, thanks to picture frame molding and paneling details on the walls and a herringbone-patterned white oak floor. It was important for our client to have a fireplace in the bedroom, so we designed a custom plaster fireplace with a fluted chimney and herringbone tile in the firebox.

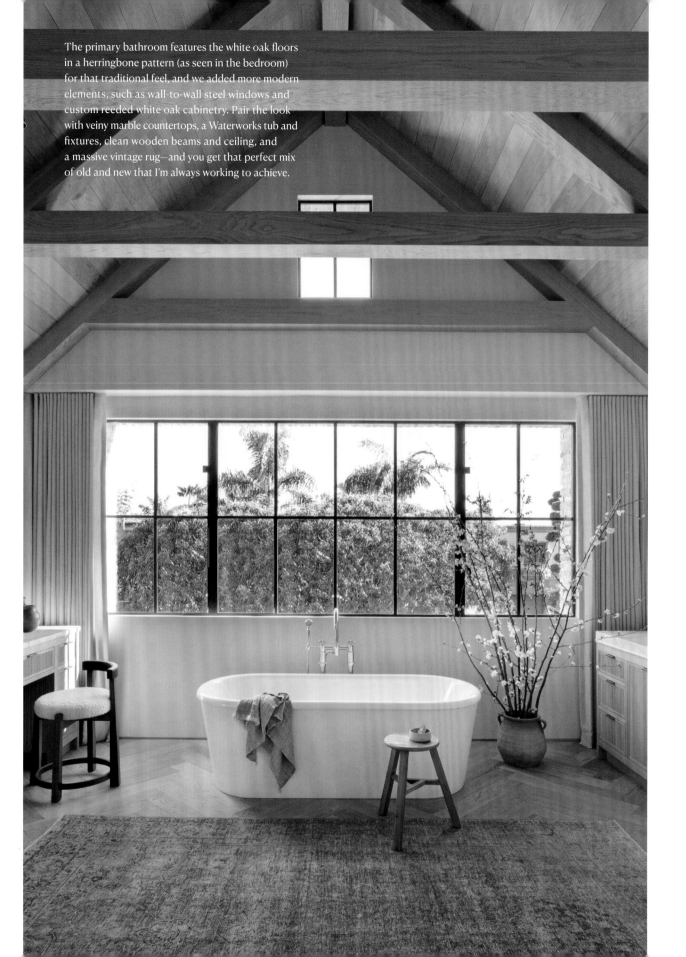

The primary bathroom features the white oak floors in a herringbone pattern (as seen in the bedroom) for that traditional feel, and we added more modern elements, such as wall-to-wall steel windows and custom reeded white oak cabinetry. Pair the look with veiny marble countertops, a Waterworks tub and fixtures, clean wooden beams and ceiling, and a massive vintage rug—and you get that perfect mix of old and new that I'm always working to achieve.

Here's a close-up of the custom reeded white oak cabinetry with veiny marble countertops and inset mirrors lined with antiqued brass, for a clean and modern look.

ABOVE AND OPPOSITE
We wanted this teenager's room to feel relevant for
years and years. We kept the tone neutral but added
functional elements like fabric Roman shades and
a built-in desk for studying. Over in the bathroom,
we added cool details like leather handles and woven
cane on the cabinet doors.

PREVIOUS PAGES
The shower in the primary bathroom is its own work
of art: a mix of steel doors, reeded glass, and fluted
marble lining the walls. It is one of the first times we
tried this combination, and it just works.

The outdoor space on the rooftop is the ultimate beachside chill zone. Part of it is designed for lounging (with flanking built-in desks that will hopefully encourage the kids to do their homework!); the other side is for bar nights and pool table hangs with the adults. We designed the bathroom to be extra durable and outdoor friendly.

TAKE THE FLOOR

The many options for flooring can feel overwhelming. I tend to stick to a few tried-and-true materials that can look drastically different depending on the style of the home. In general, flooring materials should be sturdy and able to withstand the wear and tear of . . . well, walkin' and stompin' around! I pretty much use two types of flooring: wood and stone. They are not only beautiful but also durable. Here's a bit more on each material:

· **Wood.** When sourcing wood flooring, I usually opt for reclaimed oak. There is something about the patina it develops over time that makes it look worn in the perfect way. I also love the feel of wood—it offers up just the right amount of hominess I am always trying to achieve. I get asked a lot about the width of planks, and my answer is that there is no "right" width. For my own home, I went with planks of three different widths, a choice I found funky, different, and cool. Finally, as I've mentioned, and even though it's sometimes frowned upon, I am 100 percent here for putting wood floors in a bathroom. The fear is that the wood will get moldy, but I promise, with a little extra caretaking, it's nothing you can't handle.

· **Stone.** I gravitate toward terra-cotta tiles or brick and rustic limestone, usually with tumbled edges or cobblestone pavers. We often see these in mudrooms and laundry rooms and in kitchens and bathrooms, too. Because stone is sturdy and works great when heated (hello, mountain homes), I recommend it for a home's high-traffic areas. It brings a rustic feel to any space and is a great material to mix in to moderate the prevalence of wood throughout the house.

CLOCKWISE FROM TOP LEFT
A few of my favorite flooring materials: hand-painted ceramic oval tile; Roman thin brick next to reclaimed barn wood; mixed-width white oak flooring; and super durable Blue Chinois cobblestone.

MOUNTAIN GETAWAYS

I crave the change of seasons and am addicted to what I call my "fall feeling," which is basically any type of chill in the air or excuse to bust out the sweaters. That's when I want to spark up a wood-burning fire and breathe in fresh air sprinkled with the scent of snow. I know I'm romanticizing the cold here, but when you live in a city like L.A. where the temps never dip below freezing, experiencing these changes can be magical.

That's why, when Amber Interiors was asked to work with two clients, each with a home in the mountains—one in North Carolina, the other in Montana—I jumped at the opportunity to come up with my take on a mountain getaway. With these homes, there was so much we could do that we hadn't tried before.

This chapter focuses on the decisions we made for two houses, both with designs that emphasized a strong connection to their mountain environment. In any home I work on, I want the clients to feel their surroundings—and by that, I quite literally mean they should have a strong sense of the outside environment even when inside their home. Most of the houses highlighted in this book are located in perfectly temperate California, where you can get that indoor/outdoor feeling at any time of the year. But for these clients, we had to pivot, and our design and architectural planning changed drastically. Materials matter, and throughout these next pages, you'll see why.

The exterior of our North Carolina project, designed and built with the architecture team at PLATT and the builders at Sadlon and Associates.

CLIENT: GOING TO CAROLINA

This home is tucked away in the lush mountains of North Carolina, surrounded by rolling hills dotted with more trees than I've ever seen. I had no idea about this hidden pocket of the state before this job, and at times, while designing this space, part of me wondered why I hadn't already picked up and moved here.

Built with entertaining, gathering, and escape in mind, this home is a peaceful reprieve for my New York City–based clients from the city's hustle-bustle. We needed to design a home that was comfortable and could flex with the seasons, stylistically speaking, whether in summer or winter. To bring this project across the finish line, we collaborated closely with the architecture team at PLATT and with builders Sadlon and Associates. Our collective goal was to give this space real-life tree house vibes. (I am not exaggerating when I say this house is literally surrounded by trees.) So, we set about bringing in the most complementary materials, colors, and furnishings to achieve that goal.

To truly nail the tree house aesthetic, we incorporated lots of wood, paneling, stone, and plaster on the walls, calling out, by design, one specialty material on nearly every wall. With the exception of the ceilings and some of the guest room baths, no basic paint finish was selected. As you will see when perusing the images for this project, this deliberate use of natural materials is what gave the home that desired cabin-in-the-woods quality and made a massive impact on its overall feel. We worked with a lot of reclaimed wood, which happens to be one of my favorite materials for bringing texture and character to any space. Also, several of the rooms in the house incorporated the most beautiful reclaimed wood beams to frame the ceiling, walls, and windows. These helped tie together the home's unique architectural elements and tell a cohesive story.

The great room possesses everything you might dream of for a mountain home. Not only do the floor-to-ceiling windows look out onto a sea of trees, but the hand-hewn beams we used

to line the ceilings, windows, and hallway make our clients feel as if they were out there under the tree branches. Even though the room is tall and expansive, it doesn't feel that way when you are in it. It was our goal to make this common area as cozy as could be, yet spacious enough to accommodate everyone.

We decided to use this great room as both living room and dining room, both of which have plenty of seating. Because this room is flooded with natural light, and because we chose a light-colored plaster for the walls, we opted for a richer, deeper color palette for the furniture and fixings to really ground the space. Now all you need do is imagine spending the holidays here beneath an eighteen-foot-tall Christmas tree while gazing out onto a snow-covered paradise. Sounds like my version of heaven!

When I talk about this house being designed with entertainment in mind, I am referring to the kitchen and indoor/outdoor porch. This kitchen is large and in charge, with lots of cabinet space, a huge island, and high ceilings. To me, this room is the heartbeat of the home. The clients are a young family with small kiddos full of energy, so we needed to create space for the kids to run around, a room where everyone, including friends and extended family, could gather. Whether you are whipping up a meal at the stove, drinking a margarita in the kitchen seating area, or chilling on the porch, you still feel you're near the action.

The covered porch, right off the kitchen and separated from the interior space by floor-to-ceiling pocket doors, is an entertainer's dream. We designed this space (in partnership with the architects and builders) to be used year-round. It is entirely enclosed in screens to keep the bugs away in summer, and we installed heaters galore (plus a fireplace) for the colder seasons. We hung several gas lanterns from the ceiling (my personal favorite for the space) and added comfy rocking chairs facing the view, a barbeque area for summer cookouts, and a long table for all to gather for meals.

The pantry alone deserves a standing ovation. We settled on a U-shaped butler's-style pantry with two entrances and lots of storage. The U-shape created a small alcove, which we filled with seating. The steel pantry doors and transom windows were created by highly skilled local metalworkers. This space was quite a feat to achieve, and we love how it brought charm and uniqueness to the home's hub. It also added that touch of funk we felt that the space was calling for. We made sure the pantry was functional and that all the kitchen necessities were hidden away in cabinetry but easily accessible—cue the cutest custom ladder there ever was—and we even added built-in wine storage and ice machines because . . . of course!

The kitchen's design elements are earthy, durable, and on theme with the entire project. We created a showstopper of a range hood, working with the contractor to produce one in reclaimed wood. The contractor understood that the piece needed to feel vintage, as if we had merely stumbled upon it in a magical, dilapidated European barn. (This effect is not always easy to achieve, and I must stress again the importance of assembling a good team.) The La Cornue range in brass and black enamel was on the clients' short list of what they really wanted for a kitchen. I think it helps bring even more attention to the bespoke range hood. As for the kitchen seating area, we wanted this space to feel charming and inviting, so we used a beautiful blue-green linen to cover the couch, added a round vintage wood coffee table and some sculptural vintage chairs, and hung a set of vintage mushroom paintings we found while sourcing pieces in Round Top, Texas.

Using deep hues and raw materials for this great room helps keep the focus on the view through the windows.

The kitchen features a massive island to fit the entire
family and to welcome friends to gather around,
along with a loungey seating area to hang in while
meals are being prepared.

The range hood is made from reclaimed wood, which ties together our entire vision of making this home feel earthy and durable. We chose Shaded White paint from Farrow & Ball for the perimeter cabinetry and hung two large-scale Ann Morris station pendants in an antique brass finish to match the scale and height of the ceilings.

This U-shaped butler-style pantry has two entrances with a cozy seating area in between. For a touch of modern, we chose steel pantry doors and transom windows—the only instance where we used darker steel in the entire home. The pantry is large and functional, and it's meant to be a statement piece in the kitchen.

We lined the hallway leading into another wing of the home (where the primary bedroom and offices are located) with windows facing the front of the home, which is tucked away in the mountains with trees galore. We added café curtains to soften the space and a row of vintage pendant lights that creates the perfect ambient lighting when turned on just after sunset.

This powder room is tucked away just off the hallway before you get to the primary suite (as seen at right). The entire room, from the floors to ceiling to walls, is covered in reclaimed wood, and the variation in wood tones brought an added layer of depth. We included a massive honed Carrara marble sink, a vintage mirror, and sconces with fabric shades to soften all the wood.

LATHER, RINSE, REPEAT

Sourcing vintage sinks and unique materials for sink basins is one of the best ways to set apart a powder room, or any room for that matter, from the rest of a home. A sink can oftentimes be a statement piece that can make the room. I've used everything from honed bluestone to chiseled limestone to copper, and they always get attention.

Imagine waking up surrounded by lush green trees in the summer and snow-covered ones in winter. Well, that's what my clients get to experience every morning (and I am not *not* at all envious). This room was furnished with the coziest materials—from the bed's bouclé-upholstered headboard and footboard to the thick linen-wool drapes on the windows—and we incorporated the prettiest earthy colors in shades from rust to mustard. The primary bathroom was designed with ultimate relaxation in mind. We were able to take advantage of some unused wall space to create built-in shelving, which was ideal for housing the bits and pieces our clients use in the tub. To finish the space off, we installed sweet, checked café curtains for the window.

Though this is technically a vacation home, let's be real: Our clients still had to get some work done there. So, we designed his and her offices and chill zones catered to each of them. Both his and hers spaces are on the home's top floor, under the roof, and the beautiful A-frame shape their ceilings form lends itself perfectly to the room's cozy cabin-like feel. We also designed countertops in reclaimed wood and built-ins with little nooks for all the bar necessities. Oh, and books, too! For the furnishings, we went with espresso-colored leather and ebonized oak. Not a bad place to down a whiskey on the rocks while playing a round of chess.

Down the hall, in the "hers" space, you'll find quite the opposite chill. For this mama, the room represents a true reprieve. She wanted her own little hideaway nook, a peaceful place to relax, where she could curl up and read a book or . . . hell, just take a nap! We kept this built-in space bright and light by incorporating soft fabric and pulling in pretty patterns on everything from lamp shades and armchairs to pillows and ottomans. We gave the room a special bar area with wood countertops, unlacquered brass plumbing, and cabinetry to hide glassware and a secret beverage fridge, and we sourced some copper-and-brass pendant station lights to hang down the center of the room.

On the lower floor of the house are a few more bedrooms, another family/TV room, and a seating area.

We wanted our clients' guests to feel they were on vacation throughout the home—and this was especially true for the guest room. Here, we went for a rich color palette with deep burgundy-and-espresso-colored leather and a mix of vintage furniture and new. In the guest bathroom, we used reclaimed wood for the cabinets and drawers and kept the space bright and airy.

But wait! There's more! Apart from the guest room in the main part of the house, there's also an entire *wing* for out-of-towners who make the trek to this magical home. This "guesthouse" was designed so that visiting family and friends could feel they had their own private space. It is split up into multiple parts—with a communal seating area, a small kitchen, and a dining space with windows looking out on the most epic view of the trees and mountains. We carried the design elements from the main house throughout this wing, with paneling; lots of patterns in the curtains, rugs, pillows, and other materials; and an overall breezy vibe.

The bedrooms, which flank the kitchen and main seating area, were meant to house a family easily. We called one of the guest rooms, across the space's entry hall, the Camp Room.

We are all so proud of the work we did on this lovely family home. It met the homeowners' expectations and will last for generations to come.

The primary suite is layered in the most luscious fabrics and textiles, from thick linen wool drapes in the perfect mustard color to the ivory bouclé upholstered bed. Floor-to-ceiling windows surround the enclave, and the long bench is the perfect nook to take in nature. No matter summer or winter, it's magical all year round.

To preserve the theme, we carried over the wall paneling from the bedroom into the primary bathroom. We added sconces in between inset mirrors framed with antiqued brass, built a custom door for the shower, and chose to design a built-in tub for an optimal layout.

BELOW AND OPPOSITE

This "man cave" can be found upstairs behind a hidden door in the husband's office. The entire space was covered in reclaimed wood. We found a vintage copper ship light to hang over the game table, which created the perfect whiskey and game zone.

NEXT PAGES

Over in "her" zone, we designed the ultimate room for this mama to relax in, with the coziest fabrics and a mini bar with wood countertops and unlacquered brass plumbing.

BELOW AND OPPOSITE
The incredible guest wing, or "guesthouse," as we call it, where visiting family and friends can have their own private apartment, complete with two bedrooms, two baths, a kitchenette, and dining and lounge areas.

NEXT PAGES
This guest-wing bedroom was fun to whip together. We wanted to give kids those gone-away-to-camp vibes and inspire their thirst for adventure. When planning, we decided to make it feel youthful but not childish, with bright color, texture, art, and patterns galore.

DRESSED TO IMPRESS

Aside from paint, I often get asked about window treatments. So, let's dive right into when to use different types of treatments, the seemingly million and one fabric options, the proper height for their installation, and where they should hit at the bottom:

· **Roman shades (top).** I think it's safe to say I have incorporated Roman shades into every project I have ever designed. They are the perfect layer to add to any room—which is why you often see me combining Roman shades with curtains, one of my favorite ways to mix patterns and colors in one confined space. Your eye gets drawn to the mix.

· **Café curtains (bottom left).** This is one of the sweetest additions you can make to any space. I've hung these in breakfast nooks, hallways, bathrooms, kitchens—you name it. Café curtains are one of those elements that make a space feel a bit more charming and rustic but with a dash of that traditional, European vibe I am always trying to re-create.

· **Full-length drapery (bottom right).** This is the most common style, with so many ways to do it—but you've gotta nail it. And length is key. Here is my general rule, even though I don't really believe in rules: I like drapery to just hit the floor. So, the length of drapery in each space will differ. Also, fun fact: You need to take into consideration climate and fabrics. For example, humidity can stretch out fabrics. For rod heights, I like to install them closer to the ceiling to give the illusion that the windows are slightly taller, but not so close that it looks odd. Depending on the space's overall height, I'd say install a rod about eight to twelve inches above the window. Again, that's a guesstimate but a good start.

CLIENT: AMBER'S MONTANA EXTRAVAGANZA

This is one of those homes that pretty much has it all—but it is its location that really takes the prize. Nestled in the Rocky Mountains of Montana, on the northwest corner of Yellowstone National Park, this beautiful house boasts views of tree-lined Lone Peak Mountain. Here—unlike in relentlessly summery California—residents enjoy the full complement of seasons. So, when it was time to photograph this project, we made sure to do so when snow was on the ground.

The community in which this property is located sells the lots to buyers, and then, typically, local architects and builders get involved to complete the project. We stepped in during the project's framing stage and were thus in time to choose all the materials (a combination of plaster, wood, and stone for the walls) and finishes, add architectural details, and design a unique staircase railing and rug runner. Because this is a vacation house for the clients and is located in rugged, sometimes snowy or muddy, nature, we wanted to use durable fabrics and furniture pieces that were not too precious. We knew we could have more fun selecting furnishings and fabrics with a specifically "mountain" feel. Think plaids and checks; moody, dark accent colors; and graphic Moroccan and Turkish rugs throughout. We designed the space to feel like it could transition easily from summer to winter. We wanted to evoke the feeling of being surrounded by nature whether it was sunny outside or snow was falling.

The moment you set foot in this entryway, it's impossible to ignore the epic mountain views through the expanse of windows throughout the living space. This was a big house with extremely high ceilings, which we highlighted with wood-clad beams and beautiful stacked stone fireplace surrounds. We wanted the spaces to communicate a bit more rusticity, so we affixed hand-hewn beams to the cased openings separating the various living spaces and hallways, for an added interesting layer. We also clad the ceilings in vintage barn wood.

The home had a large, open floor plan into which we had to fit a dining set and a living room large enough for a number of guests to dine comfortably. In the main living and dining room we decided against adding decorative light fixtures, to avoid creating any visual distraction from the views directly outside. Instead, we went all out with some gorgeous vintage lighting in the entryways, hallways, and kitchen and spilling out into the main living area. The private family room, just off the dining area, was made to feel inviting—the perfect spot for lounging or curling up next to the fire. Everything about the furnishings in these living spaces was chosen with comfort and relaxation in mind. I'm talking deep seats upholstered in soft, rich textures.

The kitchen was small but mighty. We aimed for designing a space with enough storage, but not so much that there would be too many empty drawers. The room's main role was as a gathering place after a day spent on the slopes or fishing in the river, a place to whip up a meal or pour a glass of wine. This space had to be highly functional, as lots of children and guests would be in and out of it. So, we opted for beautiful yet sturdy oak with a natural clear finish for all the cabinetry. We chose a reliable countertop with a chiseled edge for a more rustic touch and added a bit of charm by lining the glass pantry doors with chicken wire. The pair of vintage milk glass pendants we chose for over the island are huge, which plays with the room's scale in a fun and interesting way. We chose smaller hanging fixtures for around the space to try something different from the traditional recessed can lighting option. Overall, this kitchen is the central hub for family and friends to gather and a space that can handle wear and tear for years to come.

This great room is all about the views, and we wanted the clients to be able to take it all in from any seat. Even though the ceilings are vaulted, which could veer cold in this high-altitude home, we grounded the entire space by upholstering the deepest and comfiest seats with warm and soft fabrics. The dining room is part of the open layout, and we chose a mix of patterned and checked fabrics on the chairs to continue the cozy vibe from the lounge area.

The sitting room is just off the dining room and provides a bit more privacy and equally as much comfort as the great room. There are fireplaces galore throughout the home, and this private room was no exception.

What do you get when you add giant clear-glass doors to stunning mountain views, a stacked stone fireplace, layers of warm-toned bed and drapery fabrics, and a soft, fluffy rug? Why, a picture-perfect primary bedroom made for snoozing in, that's what! When pulling this room together, we wanted the space to feel tonal in color, but very textural, with a statement pattern to bring in a bit of the mountain theme. We chose a chocolate-brown upholstered bed with soft, curved lines on the head and footboards. You may have noticed in previous sections that I love a chaise longue in a bedroom. Here, we went with a piece with a more traditional silhouette, with tufting and exposed turned-wood legs, upholstering it in mink-colored mohair. The rug is a shaggy wool that absorbs sound and brings in a visually interesting and cozy textural layer. I knew I wanted there to be some type of pattern in the space, and I waffled over my target: Did the bed need the pop or the chaise or the window coverings? You will see that the window coverings won out—and I am obsessed with the end result. We used a bit of plaid throughout the house, and adding it to the primary bedroom helped tie this space in with the others. When planning a project, I love repeating a decorative element to tell a story.

In the primary bathroom, we lined all the walls with reclaimed wood, tying in more of the architectural elements scattered throughout the house. The heated floors are of beautiful, reclaimed French limestone with various tones of gray and brown. As for the vanities, this may seem "extra," but I had such a specific vision of what they should be, and I was so worried that our craftsman wouldn't be able to get the European vibe I so badly wanted that we sourced a vendor out of the Netherlands. They were able to nail it, realizing our vision of custom bathroom vanities with reclaimed pine wood and integrated bluestone sinks and countertops. I make no secret of my love for metal tones, and I have a tendency to pair finishes like oil-rubbed bronze and brass or copper. We wanted the tub not to skew too contemporary, but to have a more eclectic, rustic feel—so, a giant copper tub was the only way to go! Copper is a stunning material to throw into

a bathroom or kitchen. A warmer-toned metal, it naturally helps soften a space. And if it is left to age untouched, the patina it develops is simply stunning. Not to mention it's completely durable and can handle heavy use. For me, the layered, earthy elements made this bathroom feel like a unique escape for our clients.

As with most spaces we create, when it came to pulling together the rest of the home, we wanted our clients and their guests to feel they could be together when they wanted to be but then be able to sneak off to their private spaces or quiet nooks when the need arose. Because this house is three stories tall, the staircase played an important role in our plan. Just because something is functional, it doesn't mean it can't be beautifully designed. The textiles on the staircase added so much texture and pattern to a functional space that normally gets overlooked, something I wasn't about to let happen in this beautiful mountain house.

Where do I even begin with the kids' bunk room? This might just be one of my favorite bunk rooms of all time. What with the reclaimed beams, plaid curtains, and wood-paneled walls, I can hardly decide which design element makes this room. And because this is a kids' room, we did not shy away from patterns, incorporating all sorts of plaids and checks throughout, including in the curtains, rug, and bedding.

OPPOSITE
The kitchen looks cut from the mountaintop, with a super durable Gris Catalan limestone countertop, knotty oak cabinets, and overgrouted stone veneer as the backsplash.

NEXT PAGES
The kitchen is small but mighty. We knew it had to be functional, but we didn't compromise on charm, so we lined the glass pantry doors with chicken wire and layered in leather counter stools as another natural element.

A small entrance welcomes our clients into one of the most relaxing parts of the home—their bedroom! We pulled out all the stops to make these hardworking clients really feel like they are on vacation, from covering the floor in the softest shaggy wool rug to including a plush chocolate-brown upholstered bed to covering the windows with plaid drapes to drive home that cabin feeling.

It's impossible to ignore the views from this bedroom, and we wanted to make sure it was framed perfectly between the plaid window coverings. We added a mink-colored mohair chaise longue in the corner, which sits beside a fireplace.

The focal point of the bathroom was the stunning freestanding copper tub. We lined the walls with reclaimed wood and laid reclaimed French limestone on the heated floors. We paired the custom reclaimed wood vanities created in the Netherlands with bluestone countertops and sinks. For the final touches, we hung fabric Roman shades in oatmeal-colored linen, layered in vintage rugs, and added a shearling stool to soften the entire space.

In this three-story home, we did not compromise on beauty when it came to the well-trafficked staircase. We pieced together mismatched vintage Turkish kilims and Persian runners to line the treads and had the iron handrails carefully wrapped in leather. This chandelier is truly a work of art. A cluster of custom alabaster-and-brass pendants on horse bit–inspired handmade chains, it hangs down two stories of the home.

LET THERE BE LIGHT

CLOCKWISE FROM TOP LEFT
A few of the standout fixtures I've loved installing over the years include: a rotating sconce with a fabric shade; a glass ambient sconce for an entryway; a moody glass orb pendant for a powder room; and an antique brass statement piece.

Lighting is crucial to the success of a space, and it's one of the things I love most about design. You can find fixtures that fade into a room and provide the necessary ambient light or one fixture that can become the centerpiece of a room. Let's take a gander at a range of lighting we installed in some of our clients' homes. From bedside sconces to powder room pendants and massive entryway chandeliers, we've done it all.

We filled this kids' bunk room to the brim with patterns—from the plaid curtains to the checker rug and the striped bedding. We kept with the cabin theme by using reclaimed beams to build out the bunk and wood-paneled walls, which made this room the perfect indoor tree house for the kids.

For the guest suite, we were all about incorporating natural materials to help visitors embrace the outdoor elements while relaxing indoors. From the leather headboard in the bedroom to the reclaimed oak in the bathroom, we made sure this room had a little of all the textures and elements found elsewhere in the home.

IN THE CHILL ZONE

We had a few family houses that wanted to design perhaps some of the most epic chill zones. I'm talking about full bars, game zones, sometimes even a movie theater, and, of course, always complete with a massive seating area. Let's check out a few, shall we?

· **For Amber's Montana Extravaganza (bottom right),** we switched up the style a bit from the rest of the house by adding a funky vintage 1970s Mario Bellini modular sofa and textured stone on the walls, helping achieve that mountain home aesthetic. Over by the bar, we added a collection of handmade Heather Levine ceramic pendants that hung above the bar, where we designed a custom steel shelf and a copper countertop.

· **For Going to Carolina (top),** we didn't compromise on making this hangout an inviting room for the kiddos and grown-ups alike. We brought in a big ole sectional and designed a massive built-in cabinetry wall with a TV hidden behind sliding cabinets for movie nights. Then we added a long table, perfect for arts, crafts, and snacks.

· **For Worth the Wait (bottom left),** this cocktail lounge in the basement bar features leather vintage club chairs, a round game table, and a built-in bookshelf to house good reads (see more of this room on page 60).

MY VERY OWN HOME

Designing a home for yourself and your family is one of those special milestones in life. It's also one of the hardest and most stressful tasks to take on. But once it's done and you see your vision come to life, it can produce the most rewarding feeling. Still, I never felt more tested than when it was time for me to choose the design elements for my own home. At so many points, I thought I would succumb to design decision fatigue. How on earth would I, someone exposed to so many design options every day, be able to choose elements I would like (and could live with) for a long while? Impossible!

I am a pretty decisive person in general, but when it came to making decisions for my own home . . . well, the client name "Me, Myself, and I Can't Make Up My Mind" says it all. I wanted this house to encapsulate so much, yet I didn't want much at all. Aside from the aesthetics, so much of this project was about creating a *feeling*.

In this section, I break down the details of how I managed to design and create my very own home, despite having an overabundance of choices at my disposal.

For my own home, I wanted to feel like I was approaching a ranch nestled somewhere between the Belgian countryside and the California coast. I love the sounds of walking on pea gravel, so I chose that for most of the front yard. The home exterior itself is made of stone from Horizon Stone in the color Hermitage and vertical plank siding in black. The incredible team at GSLA Studio put in the landscaping and made the entire property feel lush with life.

CLIENT: ME, MYSELF, AND I CAN'T MAKE UP MY MIND

In the earliest stages of designing my home, I felt it important to create something like an oasis from the hustle and bustle of a jam-packed life. I wanted a space my family and I would cherish always and in which we could grow; a place in which to unwind or be my most creative; where we could all feel grounded, safe, and secure as we started and ended our days. But when we decided to build this home, I didn't know just how important and life-altering this home-building journey would be. In the two years it took to build our home—and for two years after we moved in—just like the house, we experienced a major evolution, morphing in ways we could never have imagined and enduring enormous challenges. And we would come out of this tumultuous time with a radically different perspective on the process.

As I know well—and especially when it comes to home building—the best-laid plans can often get turned upside down. When it came to my own house, I had every intention of keeping the project on track and staying on budget. Yet, as most projects do, this one took a little longer than expected and cost a little bit more than anticipated. But as I have mentioned before, you've gotta expect this with home building. There are just too many factors at play and way too many elements out of your control. So, instead of the Christmas 2019 date we had hoped for, we ended up moving into the house in early March 2020. Yes, the same March we all now know so well—the month that changed us, the country, and the world forever. In an additional crazy twist of fate, I had also been dealt a hand in a game I was unaccustomed to playing, one that would alter my definition of "home" and force me to focus on the importance of my surroundings in a way I never thought possible.

On March 8, 2020, I was diagnosed with multiple sclerosis (MS). After a hellish few days of my being in and out of the

hospital, scared stiff about what this meant for my future, the unthinkable happened: The world shut down for the Covid-19 pandemic. Suddenly, not only did my own world as I knew it look dramatically different, but also all of us were forced to shift our perspectives on the meaning of "home." The timing was uncanny. I remember those first two weeks of March 2020 so vividly. The highs of finally moving into our finished house, a place we had spent years designing and building, were suddenly being overshadowed by a crippling fear and uncertainty over my diagnosis and the terrifying global pandemic.

I had known while I was designing this space that I wanted it to feel safe, but I never thought we would end up needing our home in the way we did. In one fell swoop, it became a place where we would not only eat and sleep but also where we would wake up daily to a precarious world. We would not leave the house for months and months, and I would need to find solace in sitting as still as possible with my new reality, learning to lean into this new normal.

Now that you have some context for how the home came to be, and the significance this period will always have in my heart, I can finally jump into the details I have been asked about for years. In the interest of transparency, I'll confess: It was quite the experience to be at once client and designer. When it came to following my own rules and selecting my team, I decided to keep it literally in the family and hired my dad as our builder. I felt so blessed with him on board and knew we would be in the best hands. Still, regardless of how secure I felt in my experience with building homes, nothing could have prepared me for creating my own. It was, without doubt, one of the most stressful experiences of my life.

But first, let's backtrack a bit.

We bought the property, a flat one-acre parcel of land, in 2016, and continued to live in our small ranch-style home for a couple years while we saved money and dreamt up the new house. Our part of California is known for its single-story ranch-style homes, so it was important to me that we not stray too far from this type of house. We had to work with the home's existing foundation, adding to the original building by creating hallways to extra rooms, opening up ceilings, and widening doorways and windows to let the natural light flood in. By creating an almost L-shaped building, we were able to better separate the bedrooms from the living spaces and build a small, private family room where we could cozy up and watch TV away from the kitchen and main living room. We wanted the house to feel like a part of the landscape, a retreat nestled within nature rather than a structure sitting apart from it. For this reason, we figured out ways to build right up to and around some big, beautiful existing trees. Now every window and door in the house looks out onto the massive yard and mature trees.

Because we were going for cozy and safe, I didn't want anything to feel overly grand—so, no enormous great room just for the sake of it. Ours was an incredibly intentional build-out, one that suited the specific needs of our smaller family. I paid close attention to ensuring that each space in the home honored function as well as form. I wanted it to be the perfect home for me and my family, designed so that everything had a place and so that it reflected how we live and entertain. Nothing too fancy, just well-thought-out rooms with a focus on simple but impactful materials and a connection to the outdoors.

Selecting the materials and architectural details was very challenging for me. How would I choose things I would like forever? How would I continue, years later, to love what I'd selected for my own home when what I did for a living was look at option after option for other people? In the end, I decided to design something that felt timeless enough to withstand years of trends by not being trendy. "Simple but special" was the name of the game. I opted to pick only a few types of materials, and when push came to shove, I went with gorgeous neutral and natural items that felt textural and interesting.

Think white oak floors, tongue-and-groove beam ceilings, and taupe Zellige tiles on the shower walls. In the kitchen, we went with a combination of painted and white oak cabinetry throughout, some interesting reclaimed white oak ceilings, and bright but veiny marble on the countertops. Add some gorgeous lighting and plaster on the walls for a touch of texture, and we achieved a winning mix. It was a combination I had used for clients time and time again, and even after numerous years of installing it, I still loved it.

So that we start at the beginning, let's discuss the front entrance and work our way around, shall we?

They say you never get a second chance to make a good first impression, so I designed our entryway to be a welcoming place for us and our friends and family. I have always loved brick, so I chose reclaimed brick for the floors there and laid it in a herringbone pattern with a soldered border to create some visual interest. As in quite a few spaces around the home, we added vertical tongue-and-groove paneling on the walls and reclaimed white oak beams and paneling on the ceilings. We repeated this combo throughout the home, creating, in the process, a formula for when and where this detail would be applied: If the ceilings were vaulted, I applied paint-grade beams and paneling. If the ceilings were flat, I applied reclaimed oak beams and paneling. Of course, the budget would not allow me to do this everywhere, so I chose only the most impactful rooms for this approach—such as my daughter Gwyneth's bedroom, the main hallways, the kitchen, the primary suite, and the main living spaces.

I went with an open-concept plan for the main area of the home so we could have one big chill zone for friends and family. (You'll see in the rest of the layout that I used lots of nooks to separate the kitchen and dining area from the living area.) The space opens up onto the big backyard and is flooded with natural light—one of the design attributes we most wanted to highlight here. I designed the windows and doors to be as large as we could go, keeping in mind that the scale needed to match the overall vibe of this charming ranch house. The original home did not have a fireplace, so we added one to the main living room. To bring wood tones into the space, I opted not to do any traditional built-in cabinetry, but instead to design freestanding pieces flanking the fireplace to house all my books and collectibles. We are a family that loves games and music, so the pieces had to include storage and places to hide record player wires. For these, I went with a combination of open and closed white oak shelving with a cerused finish.

We vacillated over adding more square footage so we could include a formal dining room, but in the end, we decided that just wasn't our vibe. We're lucky enough to live in Los Angeles, where the weather is perfect nearly 365 days a year, so we focused instead on building a large outdoor dining area to seat my massive extended family. I mentioned earlier that the existing foundation compelled us to keep some of the house's funkier layout issues. Specifically, the original kitchen was located in an odd spot and had very low windows. We decided to use the quirky height of the windows to our advantage and designed a seating area here to house a large dining table and a massive custom built-in wicker banquette. Because this space was right off the new, relocated kitchen and in the same open layout as the living room, it felt like the perfect nook to tuck in a table for hanging out and eating or watching the game while continuing, at any given moment, to engage with whatever was happening in the kitchen.

For the new kitchen, we wanted a beautiful space that would serve as both the focal point for the adjacent open area and a gorgeous backdrop for the main living room. For this reason, I had to ensure there was zero visual clutter and direct the eye to all the texture and materials in the kitchen. This was one of those instances when I thought long and hard about what elements to incorporate that would make the kitchen feel interesting and unique but not look tired in a matter of months. With long lead times, I had to make my selections early on in the building process; I knew if I didn't pull the trigger, I would be forever indecisive. So, I worked my way down a checklist, selecting those items that would become the centerpieces for the kitchen.

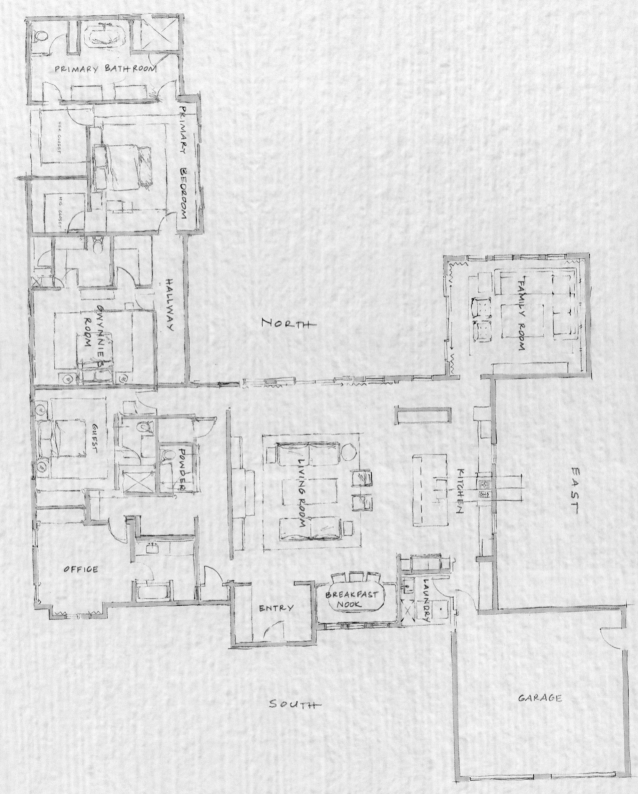

An illustrated rendering of the floor plan of my home.

No matter what, I knew the kitchen island had to be the centerpiece of the room. Originally, I hunted for a massive vintage piece I could retrofit to accommodate my sink, dishwasher, trash can, and so on—but this was not as easy as I had hoped it would be. When I realized I might have to give up my search, I started reaching out to my tried-and-true vendors. I had ordered from and been a fan of the work of UK antiques dealer Matthew Cox. I was perusing his site one day when I saw the most covetable piece of furniture, something I just had to have. I contacted him immediately and asked if he would partner with me to design the perfect custom-built island based on that piece. He let me know he had done it before and agreed. It took a while, and shipping cost a pretty penny, but it was worth it to obtain such a stunning addition to the space.

When it came to selecting the cabinetry style, I knew I wanted simple. I love to collect things but did not want the visual clutter a collection can bring, so I designed a shelving unit with sliding doors; the rippled-glass panels made the items stacked behind them essentially disappear. You will notice that I created counter-to-ceiling cabinets—called appliance garages—which hide all the small appliances and knick-knacks that tend to clutter counters. (Anytime you can use this style of cabinet, I say go for it!) When it came to choosing a color, I went with a neutral greige.

As designers, we can feel inundated by all the available styles out there. By the time I created my own vent hood, I had sourced inspiration for my *clients'* kitchen hoods for years. So, how was I going to choose something special enough for my *own* kitchen? Welp!

Then, one evening, I was eating in an Italian restaurant and noticed that the pizza oven in the back was completely tiled from floor to ceiling. Though it was a look I had no doubt seen a hundred times before, it got me thinking about how this particular detail could be applied to my own kitchen. That's when the penny dropped for me, and the all-tile hood and backsplash for my home were born. Covering these items with tile was a way to do something different, to introduce texture to the space. I went with Zellige tiles in Weathered White, which jibed perfectly with the greige-colored cabinetry and gorgeous, warm-veined marble I chose for the countertops and partial backsplash.

Because there were flat ceilings in here, I followed my formula and added the same beautifully textured reclaimed white oak beams I'd used elsewhere. You'll notice I chose *not* to put any pendants above the kitchen island—this was a shocker to some, but with all the other interesting elements happening in the space, I didn't feel they were needed. (I don't like to add things just because they're popular.) Still, I did have the wiring installed for them, on the off chance I change my mind one day.

I've wanted a range from the French brand Lacanche for as long as I can remember. Without hesitation, I knew I couldn't go wrong with the black-and-brass combo. (By the way, this rule holds true for most things. Whether it's outfits, cars, or watches, black and brass will never fail you.)

267

The cabinets were designed to reach to the ceiling and to house all my appliances behind sliding doors. The color is one of my favorite greiges, Figueroa, by Portola Paints and Glazes.

The focal point of the kitchen is the island, which I had initially envisioned sourcing as a vintage piece, but I couldn't find something large enough. So I ended up working with one of my tried-and-true vendors, Matthew Cox, from the UK, to create this big beauty.

I designed this custom wicker banquette to look like a church pew, which gives the lines great curvature, but I also wanted it to be extremely comfortable, so we made a cushion with a simple French seam and minimal tufting and, of course, loads of plush pillows. I added brass sconces with a gorgeous patina and a few vintage Charlotte Perriand chairs to wrap around the other side of the table.

The family room features thick dark-green velvet blackout drapes to help frame the windows and create the ultimate atmosphere for TV watching.

I mentioned earlier that we wanted a family room that felt a bit more removed from the rest of the main living spaces. We built ours just off the new kitchen, in a void between the house's original footprint and a giant existing oak tree we wouldn't dare touch. The room sits right under the oak, and we added a wall of windows looking out on it—turning the family room into a beautiful space flooded daily with natural light. This space was meant for chillin' hard, so I designed a really comfortable, deep modular sofa we could all sink into while watching TV. I added all sorts of vintage furniture and finally got to use a piece I had been saving until I found the perfect place for it: a giant vintage French baker's table bought years ago in Texas.

Now that we've walked through the communal wing of the home, let's move on to the snooze wing.

I wanted all the bedrooms to be on one side of the house, mainly to keep some separation between our private spaces and the areas that guests frequented. The house's L-shape really emerged with the design of the window-lined hallway. The almost floor-to-ceiling glass looks onto the patio, which features a beautiful stone trough fountain and a lush green planter bed.

As with the rest of the home, we didn't want the primary bedroom to be overly grand or large. Our job here was really about nailing down a cozy atmosphere that required only the true essentials. As with the whole house, this space looked straight out from the bed onto our yard, so we could see all the greenery and those big, mature oaks. Pretty picturesque, if you ask me!

In my primary bathroom, I carried on the theme of simple, classic materials and architectural details, for cohesion with the rest of the home. You'll see here again the reclaimed white oak beams on the ceiling, Calacatta marble on the vanities, and more white oak cabinetry for the vanities and storage. For the countertops, I designed a unique ogee edge detail to accompany the large sink with its five-inch front apron, inspired by an old Belgian bathroom I once saw in a book on European farmhouses. It was such an

exceptional design that I knew I wanted to incorporate it in a bathroom. For this one, I changed the details a bit and came up with a version more tailored to my style and needs. There was a perfect alcove for the Empire tub from Waterworks, with its unlacquered Waterworks brass plumbing fixtures. For privacy and aesthetics, I added sheer linen café curtains to the window behind the tub.

We had enough room in the space to include a water closet and a large shower. I didn't want the shower door to be anything too basic, so I reached out to a metal fabricator and designed a powder-coated steel shower door. As much as I love wooden floors in the bathroom, we needed a happy mix of materials here, so I chose limestone to break up all the pretty white oak and reclaimed beams. Last but not least, I designed a built-in vanity with plenty of storage for all my bits and bobs.

Now, let's move on to my favorite teenager's room! I wanted this room to be all about Gwyneth, so I let her take over the reins in choosing the details. She wanted her room to be different from the rest of the house, so she chose a "really cool" wallpaper, watercolor-esque in a pretty blue and gray. She also wanted her room to be colorful, with lots of patterns, but not too girly or youthful, so she chose to add a layer of pattern by way of curtains in a slightly more sophisticated floral motif. We included vintage furniture pieces, a vintage chandelier, and a very comfortable bed, and this tween was as happy as could be.

For G's bathroom, we wanted the same youthful-but-not-too-kidlike vibe. Gwyneth had a big hand in selecting the materials here, too, and she chose Zellige shower tile in a fun herringbone pattern, in Weathered White, and a coordinating herringbone pattern for the brick floor. We went with a powder-coated custom shower door in a greige, a pretty brass pivoting mirror, brass sconces, and Waterworks for all the plumbing. By adding high paneling that rose three-fourths of the way up the wall, we elevated the room, giving the walls and overall aesthetic a more polished feel.

Last but not least, let's talk about the guest bathrooms and the powder room. Truth be told, they are some of my favorite rooms in the house. Starting in the powder room, we have the vintage vanity and sink, both of which make my heart skip a beat. I was originally looking for a vintage carved Bluestone sink to mount to the wall, but in my search, I stumbled upon quite the score: this vintage vanity from Belgium. When I got the dimensions from my vendor and realized it was a perfect fit, I squealed with joy. The deep gray soapstone sink with its bright veining provides just the right mood. I loved pairing this with the reclaimed brick on the floor, and I changed up the way the floors were laid out by selecting a basketweave pattern.

Because I crave vintage, and the powder room had no windows, I leaned into the moody European vibe with an antique gold-gilt French mirror I picked up on a sourcing trip. The found vintage sconces were a tragic, but ultimately very happy, accident, as the original sconces I had selected for the home were accidentally thrown away. It still hurts to talk about, but I feel as though the ones I ended up using were ten times more beautiful anyway.

For one of the guest bathrooms, I wanted anyone who used it to feel immersed in an intentional room design, so we spared no expense. I elevated the space with the custom glass-and-brass shower enclosure, the vintage tumbled limestone floors, and my trusty Zellige tiles in Weathered White. I kept the vanity in a natural white oak and added the reeded door and drawer details to give it some interest. I topped it all off with a Calacatta marble slab countertop and unlacquered brass plumbing on shower and sink.

And that is it, my very own home project, detailed right down to the who, what, where, when, and why. It is a project I will forever be proud of, and I am so happy my family can call this place home, whether it's for a few years or forever. The memories here will be ones I'll never, ever forget.

OPPOSITE
I carried the same beams from the kitchen into this hallway, to keep in theme and follow my formula for flat ceilings. I also added three vintage pendants I had been dying to install in my own home for years. These substantial pieces really steal the show in this hallway, which is exactly what I wanted them to do.

NEXT PAGES
To keep it quiet and comfy, my bedroom features only the essentials. I brought in all sorts of textures with the must-have furniture—the bouclé-upholstered bed, the rusty velvet chaise longue—and textured, sandy linen fabric for the drapery.

BELOW AND OPPOSITE
This bathroom is all about the classic materials: Cala-catta marble, reclaimed white oak, brass plumbing, and limestone floors.

NEXT PAGES
My daughter, Gwyneth, chose all of the details for her bedroom and bath design. I think she nailed it. Her suite has color and texture and is timeless enough that she'll be happy with it into her teenage years.

We designed the backyard for hanging out with lots
of grass for my kiddo and animals to run wild and
free. I carried the same stone from the exterior of
the main home to the outdoor fireplace and built
a pergola with reclaimed wood and vintage pendants.
Our property is framed by beautiful oak trees, so
I wanted to keep the backyard earthy and tonal to
feel as if we're removed from the city.

TILE STYLE

There are plenty of ways to slice and dice tile patterns and configurations, so let's break down the different ways you can lay out these materials:

- **Herringbone (top right).** Use this configuration for a traditional European-style look.

- **Staggered (top left and bottom left).** For a clean, modern look, go for this approach, traditionally used with subway tile, a staple of prewar Manhattan apartments.

- **Basketweave (bottom right).** This pattern especially looks good with handmade tile, lending a more textured look.

ACKNOWLEDGMENTS

When I was diagnosed with multiple sclerosis in early 2020, the fear and uncertainty of it forced me to look within and work to overcome my limitations. I believe that being surrounded by so much love and such a strong support system is why I was able to dig deep and find the strength to shift my perspective and live a life full of gratitude and purpose. I am forever grateful for the chance to recalibrate my intentions and focus on all the beautiful parts of my life.

And so to have been given the opportunity to write another book is one that I will never take for granted. To have the space and platform to reflect on my career and elaborate on the hows and whys of what I do reminds me that I'm lucky to call Interior Design my job. I am on a wild ride and a unique journey, and without the support of so many people, none of it would be possible.

First and foremost, I want to thank my family. Mom, Dad, Ryan and Tess, Lyndsie and Brendan, Granny, and all my nieces and nephews, thank you for filling my life with so much love and support.

To the talented and hardworking people who made every single thing you see in these pages possible, I owe so much to you. For every skill I lack, you all do it and exceed my expectations with ease.

Angelin and Nicole, thank you for believing in me enough to give me another shot at this whole book-writing thing. I am honored you have invested so much time and energy into making our second book together a reality. I look forward to many more. And to everyone at Potter—specifically, Darian Keels, Robert Diaz, Terry Deal, Kim Tyner, Allison Renzulli, and Jana Branson—you are the A team and I'm proud to have you work on my book.

Shade, your eye for beauty and your unwavering talent is remarkable. Shooting this book with you was an experience unlike any other. I am forever grateful our paths crossed.

Cat "Kitty" Chen, whoops we did it again. I adore you and am forever in debt at your willingness to go on this journey with me. I look forward to doing this over and over again. Cheers to you.

Katie "Khatie" Kelly, you are truly the most magical gem of a human. Thank you for bringing this book to life with your incredible energy and amazing gifts.

Mike, thank you for cheering me on no matter how hard the road to get here has been. Your partnership and support through it all mean everything to me.

Gwyneth, you are my light. You are my soul. You are my everything. You have given me the gift to live my life with a true purpose. Your spirit and strength day in and day out inspires me to be the best version of myself. I love you beyond words.

RESOURCES

Pages 28–61
Architect: Bob Newlon
Builder: Brad Van
Plumbing: Waterworks
Tile: Eco Outdoors,
Exquisite Surfaces, Country
Floors, Ann Sacks
Paint: Portola Paints
Flooring: Custom
French Oak
Lighting: Vintage, Ann
Morris, Rose Tarlow
Furniture: Vintage, Shoppe
Amber Interiors

Pages 64–97
Builder: Ingenuity Builders
Plumbing: Waterworks,
Devol, Barber Wilson
Tile: Exquisite Surfaces,
Country Floors, Deknock
Paint: Portola Paints,
Farrow & Ball
Flooring: Custom
Lighting: Vintage, Obsolete,
Matthew Cox
Furniture: Vintage, Shoppe
Amber Interiors

Pages 98–111
Builder: Gunn Construction
and Building
Plumbing: Waterworks
Tile: Arto Brick, Cle Tile,

Tabarka, Mission Tile West
Paint: Portola Paints, Dunn-
Edwards, Farrow & Ball
Flooring: Custom
Lighting: Vintage, Mullan,
O'Lampia Studio, Obsolete
Furniture: Vintage, Shoppe
Amber Interiors

Pages 118–163
Architect: Luca Pignata,
Backen and Backen
Builders: Stocker & Allaire
Plumbing: Waterworks,
Rocky Mountain Hardware
Tile: Ann Sacks, Exquisite
Surfaces, Cle Tile
Paint: Texston Plaster
Flooring: Essex Flooring
Lighting: Vintage, Apparatus
Furniture: Vintage, Shoppe
Amber Interiors

Pages 164–187
Architect: Eric Olsen Design
Builder: Longman
Construction
Plumbing: Waterworks
Tile: Exquisite Surfaces,
Cle Tile, Ann Sacks,
Zellij Gallery
Paint: Portola Paints, Farrow
& Ball, Dunn-Edwards
Flooring: Custom

Lighting: Vintage, Allied
Maker, Holly Hunt,
Anna Karlin
Furniture: Vintage, Shoppe
Amber Interiors

Pages 192–225
Architect: PLATT US
Builders: Sadlon
and Associates
Plumbing: Waterworks,
Devol
Tile: Exquisite Surfaces,
Architectural Ceramics,
Tabarka, Ann Sacks,
Country Floors
Paint: Portola Paints,
Farrow & Ball, Sherwin-
Williams, Dunn-Edwards
Flooring: Burchette and
Burchette Hardwood Floors
Lighting: Vintage, Ann
Morris, Factory 20, Roman
and Williams Guild, Hector
Finch, O'Lampia Studio
Furniture: Vintage, Shoppe
Amber Interiors

Pages 228–251
Architect: Locati Architects
Builders: The PRG Group
Plumbing: Waterworks,
Watermark
Tile: Exquisite Surfaces,

Cle Tiles, Country Floors,
Zellij Gallery
Paint: Portola Paint, Farrow
& Ball, Sherwin-Williams,
Dunn-Edwards
Flooring: Custom
Lighting: Vintage, Obsolete,
Devol, Lumfardo, Stahl
and Band
Furniture: Vintage, Shoppe
Amber Interiors

Pages 256–283
Architect: Amber
Interiors Inc.
Builder: JR Payne
Construction
Landscape: GSLA Studio
Windows: Marvin Windows
and Doors
Plumbing: Waterworks
Countertops: Modul Marble
Tile: Cle Tiles
Paint: Portola Paints
Flooring: Duchateau
Lighting: Vintage, Shoppe
Amber Interiors
Furniture: Vintage, Shoppe
Amber Interiors

Copyright © 2023 by Amber Lewis

Photographs copyright © 2023 by Shade Degges

Photographs on pages 112 (bottom left), 141 (bottom right), 256-283 and 285 (bottom left) copyright © by Jess Isaac

Illustration on page 265 by Hilary Dempsey

Library of Congress Cataloging-in-Publication Data
Lewis, Amber, author. | Degges, Shade, photographer.
Title: Call it home : the details that matter / Amber Lewis ; photographs by Shade Degges.
Identifiers: LCCN 2022055179 (print) LCCN 2022055180 (ebook) ISBN 9780593235522 (hardcover) | ISBN 9780593235539 (ebook)
Subjects: LCSH: Interior decoration.
Classification: LCC NK2115 .L438 2023 (print) LCC NK2115 (ebook) DDC 747—dc23/eng/20221125
LC record available at https://lccn.loc.gov/2022055179
LC ebook record available at https://lccn.loc.gov/2022055180

ISBN 978-0-593-23552-2
Ebook ISBN 978-0-593-23553-9

Printed in China
Editor: Angelin Adams
Editorial assistant: Darian Keels
Designer: Robert Diaz
Production editor: Terry Deal
Production manager: Kim Tyner
Compositors: Merri Ann Morrell, Zoe Tokushige, and Hannah Hunt
Photographer: Shade Degges
Copyeditor: Jenna Dolan
Proofreaders: Elisabeth Beller, Janice Race, and Rebecca Zaharia
Publicist: Jana Branson
Marketer: Allison Renzulli

10 9 8 7 6 5 4 3 2 1

First Edition